angry.

2. angrier

3. angriest 20 hevier heavier

happy I. fa

happiest

happier

7 ez easy easy easy e
easy easy ea
e easier easier easier
easier easie
easiest easi est easue
easiest easies
9 funny easiest prett-
funnier pretty pretty
pre
pre
funniest pre

3 prity pretty pr

Insightful and candid ... written with humor and from the heart ... *An Accidental Advocate* should serve as a roadmap for other parents of exceptional children.

LORRIE GOEGAN Chair, Learning Disabilities Association of Canada

An Accidental Advocate is a phenomenal read. Kathryn Burke's relentless journey of advocacy for her son, chronicled in the book, will help professionals and those in the world of education see the 'other side.' It will also empower parents of children with exceptional needs to advocate in a collaborative manner.

LORI FANKHANEL Founder and President, SPD Canada

Every parent with a child who has learning challenges should read *An Accidental Advocate*. Kathryn's story is both personal and inspiring as she describes her journey from the joys of new parenthood, through denial that her son was experiencing more than simply short-term challenges, to embracing her role as advocate, not only for her son, but the entire LD community.

MICHELE PENTYLIUK President, Learning Disabilities Association of Alberta

This is an insightful, focused and moving account of a mother's journey through the perilous pathways and joys of parenting a child with exceptional abilities which are different from those expected of a "normal" child. So different, in fact, that they are generally labeled in terms of learning disabilities. Kathryn Burke found herself becoming an advocate, politician, writer, journalist, blogger, manager of expectations, fighter, imagineer, change agent and counsel to others in a way that she never expected. She does this work well, as all who know her know. This account is a handbook for those living through such an experience but is also a handbook for those who find themselves an accidental advocate, whatever the cause. You will laugh, cry and reflect — all a reader could ask for.

STEPHEN MURGATROYD Chief Scout, Murgatroyd Communications & Consulting Inc an accidental advocate

KATHRYN BURKE

An Accidental Advocate

A mother's journey with her exceptional son

Sextant

An Imprint of Cambridge Strategies Inc.

Library and Archives Canada Cataloguing in Publication

Burke, Kathryn Louise, 1956–
An accidental advocate : a mother's journey with her exceptional son / Kathryn Burke.

Issued also in electronic format.
ISBN 978-1-926755-03-8

1. Burke, Kathryn Louise, 1956–.
2. Learning disabled children — Identification.
3. Learning disabled children — Education.
4. Attention-deficit-disordered children — Identification.
5. Attention-deficit-disordered children — Education.
6. Learning disabilities.
7. Attention-deficit hyperactivity disorder.
8. Mothers of children with disabilities — Alberta — Biography.
I. Title.

LC4704.B837 2011   371.92'6   C2010-907086-0

In-house editor: Xanthe Couture
Cover and interior design: Natalie Olsen, Kisscut Design
Author photograph: Robert Bray

Sextant Publishing
Suite 208, Empire Bldg   10080 Jasper Ave
Edmonton, AB   T5J 1V9   Canada
Phone: (780) 420-0505

Printed and bound in Canada

This book is dedicated three ways:

To Paul, Colin, Kyle, Nancy, Sam and Charon (in heaven)

I love you all past Pluto!

To parents everywhere with children with exceptional learning needs

I hope this book provides you with the knowledge that you are not alone.
I wrote it for you.

To people world over who work as volunteers or in a professional capacity helping people with learning disabilities or other exceptional needs

I believe you are angels on earth.
I thank you for all that you do every day.

Contents

An Accidental Advocate

Author's preface

This book is about our journey of advocacy for our son, Colin.

Colin is intellectually gifted. He is affected by learning disabilities, specifically dysgraphia, dyslexia, and organizational challenges. He has Attention Deficit Hyperactivity Disorder (ADHD). To the best of our knowledge, he is not challenged by other neurodevelopmental or exceptional learning needs. In addition to co-existing learning disabilities and ADHD, Colin has suffered from respiratory issues throughout his life, primarily recurrent pneumonia and asthma. He was diagnosed with moderate level stuttering as a pre-schooler, a condition which has been completely remediated.

Learning disabilities refer to a number of disorders which can affect how a person acquires, organizes, retains, understands or uses verbal or nonverbal information. People with learning disabilities typically have average to above average intellect and reasoning and are fully able to learn given the right intervention. Learning disabilities range in severity and may interfere with the acquisition and use of one or more of the following:

• oral language including listening, speaking and understanding

• reading including word recognition and comprehension

• written language

• mathematics

Individuals with learning disabilities often have difficulties with organizational and social skills. The impact of learning disabilities changes over the course of a person's life. These changes are affected by a person's strengths and needs and the manner in which they interact with their environment. Learning disabilities are suspected when a person unexpectedly under-achieves at school or can only achieve with unusually high levels of effort and support.

Conservative estimates of learning disabilities place its incidence at one in every ten people. The causes of learning disabilities are unknown, although current research indicates it is a neurological condition which is also hereditary in nature. Learning disabilities are not caused by lack of motivation or poor teaching, although these factors may further complicate the challenges faced by individuals with learning disabilities.

Learning disabilities often co-exist with other neurological or health conditions, lending complexity to the issue. A common co-occurring condition is ADHD, estimated to affect approximately 50% of people with learning disabilities.

More detailed information about learning disabilities is

available on websites of Learning Disabilities Associations around the world. Of particular note are the websites of the Learning Disabilities Association of Canada and the Learning Disabilities Association of America. Other excellent resources include LDOnline, the National Centre for Learning Disabilities, and Misunderstood Minds. All sites are easily found via an online search engine. Because of the significant co-existence of learning disabilities and ADHD, most sites also include information about ADHD. The majority of these sites also contain links to local regional, provincial or state resources.

Readers wishing more information about learning disabilities and its co-existing conditions are encouraged to consult experts within their community.

Kathryn Burke
Edmonton, Alberta
January 2011

Source: Information in the Author's Preface was abstracted from the website of the Learning Disabilities Association of Canada and A Call to Action: World Summit on Learning Disabilities, December 5, 2008 which was written by Kathryn Burke for the Organizing Committee of the World Summit.

An introduction of sorts

It happened accidentally. I did not set out to be an advocate. I was going to be the president of a hospital or the CEO of some company. The latter is now true but not quite in the way my 24 year old self had envisioned.

I had excelled at university and was on the fast track to corporate success. My creative pursuits involved sketching, tailoring and other forms of art but certainly not writing. Then, life happened. My world today is dramatically different than I thought it would be. My sketchpad and sewing materials do emerge from time to time but my creative release is through writing. Most importantly of all, I am now a wife and mother of two children with exceptional learning needs. I am convinced both these roles have made me a better person.

    My 24 year old self would never have envisioned that at 53, she would write a book about a journey of advocacy for her gifted son affected by learning disabilities and ADHD. Perhaps in the arrogance of the day, she may have perceived it to be possible to have a child who was gifted. While lacking in self confidence about many things, there was one certainty for that

24 year old woman; she had some grey matter with well tuned and firing neurons. This one belief gave her resiliency. She would not have seen herself married as she had effectively given up on meeting someone. She certainly would not have predicted she would fall in love with a brilliant man who sustained a serious spinal cord injury at 13. Meeting that man was still nine years in the future for that 24 year old. She could not begin to realize how incredibly lucky she would become.

    This is the story of how I accidentally became an advocate. It is also a love story, but not in the movie theatre, "they lived happily ever after genre" with the Celine Dion sound track. It is about my unapologetic love for my sons and my husband. It is how the love of my sister and others made a difference in my life. The power of love has led me to believe it is possible to move mountains — or at least find a safe way around them.

My roots

Something quite unusual happened in the months immediately before I began writing this book. I am not sure why, but I found myself sharing aspects of my past with some friends.

It started innocently enough. When asked questions about my youth, I began answering honestly and not defaulting to the sanitized version of events I had constructed about my childhood. Perhaps my new openness was because it was safe to speak about my upbringing. My mother died four weeks after my oldest son was born. My father, seriously impacted by dementia, generally does not know who I am.

The fact that I feel my mother reaching out from the grave to control my actions, even though I am now in my fifties, hints at the fact that my childhood was a bit challenging.

I am the youngest of three girls. My sister Nancy is nearly nine years older than me. My other sister, Charon, was almost six years older; I am now the age she was when she died. When I was a toddler, my mother had a near-death experience following surgery. She had memories of looking down on the doctors and nurses as they worked on her. Nancy, who was basically my mini-mom, told me our mother was changed when she came home from the hospital. Ironically, she lost her love of life after she nearly died. With the benefit of hindsight, we both now suspect she may have suffered some brain damage.

I don't remember the mother who loved life. I just remember a controlling woman who drank everyday and told me how awful I was. Though I would not recognize it during my youth, as an adult I came to understand that I had been emotionally abused as a child. My father was nicer, but the adult me now realizes he was complicit in the abuse. He did nothing to stop it.

I was the only child at home from the age of 14. I became my mother's mother. I handled virtually all the domestic chores. My father did not do anything domestic. He worked outside the home. Period. My mother made it clear I had duties. I support children having responsibilities at home. But in this instance, it was all about scale and who was pulling the weight in our family. I did the majority of cooking, cleaning, banking, and grocery shopping, the latter impacted by how many bags I could tote home. Because my family also bred and showed dogs, there was dog duty before and after school. Shoveling poop from a litter of eight Airedales was routine. My mother consistently told me I was lazy and that I owed her as she had brought me into this world. I have vivid memories of being awoken at five am with her exclaiming, "Get your lazy bones out of bed. You think you are so smart, but you are not."

I plotted escape but wanted to be strategic about it. My

sister Charon moved out of the house shortly after our family relocated from Montreal to Calgary. I had just started high school. Charon met a man and moved with him to a small community in British Columbia. She later confessed to me that the situation at home had colored her judgment. Effectively, she was escaping our home but the consequence was a bad marriage that lasted seven years. My parents effectively disowned her and did not speak to her for almost six of those years. I have clear memories of them throwing out her Christmas gifts as she tried, unsuccessfully, to reconnect with them. Almost daily I was admonished, "Don't hurt us the way your sister did!" What that meant was that I was supposed to tow the line and do as they wanted.

Nancy married a wonderful man a month before I turned 15. They lived in Winnipeg, one time zone and an expensive long distance phone call away. As a young couple, I know they did not have a great deal of money. My new brother in law worked in banking and has always been a skilled money manager. I am certain a line item was included in their monthly budget to cover my collect long distance calls. My sister and her husband Sam were my supports, the human equivalent to life vests, in what was the sea of insanity in which I lived, alone, with several dogs and my two parents. I could not let my parents know I was calling my sister, something they would regard as being "disloyal" to them. So I called collect. It was a matter of survival.

I missed a great deal of high school. By grade eleven, my mother had established a little cottage industry. She ran a pet grooming service from our basement. She was very adept at grooming show terriers, a skill I acquired as well. She would normally groom one pet or show dog a day. But before dog shows, about once a month, that number would climb to two or three per day. I was expected to help and frequently stayed home from school to groom dogs.

The pattern of my mother's addiction was very evident. She was a tiny woman who ate little. She began drinking a double shot of rye ever hour as soon as she finished grooming a dog, about four in the afternoon. She would hide the drink when clients came to pick up their pet. The drinking would continue until about midnight at which time she would go to bed. A pack of cigarettes was always at the ready, and by the end of the day, she generally made it through that pack. Drinking on little food resulted, I am certain, in horrendous hangovers. As she took a drag on her morning cigarette, she would pop pain killers and decongestants and take those pills on a regular basis until the soothing impact of the alcohol consumed at the regular four o'clock drinking time resolved her symptoms of alcohol withdrawal.

There is a saying that it is hard to see the big picture when you are surrounded by the frame. I was unhappy during my teen years. But I did not know normal. When I was 16, an event occurred that enabled me to gain insight into the abnormal nature of my life. We travelled as a family to dog shows throughout Alberta. Normally, we would leave after my father got home from work on a Friday, and make the trek back from the show in late afternoon on a Sunday. Supper, more often than not, was on the road. One fall we were making the trip back to Calgary from an Edmonton show. The evenings had become quite cold. Mid journey, we pulled into a highway roadside restaurant where my parents had agreed to meet others travelling back from the show. My parents made me wait, in the dark, in the cold, on the side of the road, stuck in the car with the dogs while they went in, had food, and undoubtedly drank. The rationale for me staying in the car — someone had to take care of the dogs.

I remember watching the windows of the car fog up as the temperature outside dropped; I was chilled and congested with both a cold and from crying. I wondered if I should run away. But, being practical, I figured it would be stupid for a young girl to walk alone on a highway after dark. I suspected it would not end well. I stayed in the car. I recall using paper towels to tend to the natural side effects of crying for an extended period. I am not sure how long I was left alone with the dogs — likely the time it would take for a large party to order, receive and consume their food. But it felt like days. I remember choking back the takeout they bought for me as my supper meal. Something snapped for me that day, and that was a good thing. I came to the realization that what was happening to me was not normal. I needed to hang on long enough to leave on my own terms and in a way that ultimately was to my benefit. I began to think strategically. But, this use of strategy would not protect me from the emotional slings and arrows launched in my direction from my mother. It would not stop me from playing the tapes in my head that challenged my very worth as a human being.

With their success in showing dogs, our family attracted a collection of people who always seemed to be at our house. They would come to learn how to groom and show their dog. And they would drink. These frequent visitors began to notice my situation. I remember being questioned by one about why I had stayed outside in the car on that infamous night. My parents had said I *wanted* to stay out with the dogs. In some strange way, it was comforting that they had actually felt it necessary to lie about the incident. I took a risk and responded that I was made to stay in the car. I began to get quiet support. As I got older, many people from the dog community encouraged me to leave home.

There was little deviation in the pattern of my life throughout high school. Despite skipping a great deal, I graduated with high enough marks and sufficient credits to have options, including attending university. I went to my high school graduation with my friend's parents. My father did arrive in time to see the ceremony; my mother chose not to attend. I remember feeling pangs of jealousy watching how proud other parents were of their children. It was not about gifts or fireworks. It was about being valued as a person.

After high school, my mother's expectation was that I would remain at home and tend to the family business. I would continue doing what I had been doing outside school hours, but now full time. I felt trapped without a future. I had no money and no visible means of getting away. Emotionally, I was at a very low stage in my life. But, for the first time ever, I began to sense my father was uncomfortable with my situation. He suggested I needed to get out and perhaps go to university. My friends were all at the University of Calgary and I wasted no time submitting my application. I started in the winter term. Life for me never looked rosier!

Breaking away

*I loved university! I loved absolutely everything about it.
For the first time in my life, I felt free. I was empowered.
I had enough focus to get the work done and applied
myself with gusto.*

My parents paid for my books and tuition that first semester.
After that, my university education was self financed. I did
make some money from grooming and showing dogs, but
that income was unpredictable and insufficient to finance my
future. The summer after my first semester of university, I got
my first real job outside the house, providing administrative
support in a human resources office of a fertilizer plant.
My work ethic was appreciated. I was praised and gave some
thought to staying on. But in the end, I concluded I needed
to get my degree.

I decided to major in sociology. When I was reading sociology text books or doing essays, it did not feel like work. That
choice caused an immediate stir at home. It was considered a
silly subject. I was told, on several occasions, to go into education — where I would get the summers off or into nursing

which was a good job for a woman! I began to understand the underlying principles of feminism. My roles and opportunities should not be defined by gender. I was as good as anyone else, at least in theory.

University also provided me with an understanding about the profound difference one person can make in the life of another. The person in this case was Dr. Merlin Brinkerhoff, a professor in the Department of Sociology. I suspect he never knew how important he was in helping to change my life.

With my decision to major in sociology, I was required to take a full year statistics class. A high school friend also needed to take the class and we figured we would suffer through it together. I enjoyed math, but did not consider myself to be strong in the subject. There were gaps in my math education because of having skipped so much school. Yet, I found stats to be elegant, logical and straightforward — a view not shared by too many others in the class! The first lab assignment was, I now recognize, a fishing expedition on the part of our professor, Dr. Brinkerhoff, to gauge our aptitude. I invested considerable effort into that assignment. Dr. Brinkerhoff's office was on a well travelled route between the stats lab and the department coffee lounge. On my way to get a coffee before class, Merlin, as I came to know him, stopped me and asked me into his office. I did not step in with confidence. My self-esteem, though growing, was sufficiently fragile that it might have shattered with an overly negative exchange.

He first asked me why I had used some of the approaches

I had in the assignment. I explained my rationale. He then shared with me that he liked my approach. He asked me if I was in the honors program. I replied, "What is the honors program?" He then asked me if I needed a job. In shock, I told him I did. I enrolled in the honors program, became his research assistant and continued to work with him through both my undergraduate and graduate degrees. And I only got a B on that damned assignment but was one of the few to get a full A in the class!

That short discussion during the second week of my second semester of university was life altering. During my teen years, my belief in myself had eroded. The sentiment that I was smart and could succeed began to creep back into my psyche. Having the backing of someone who had independently come to the conclusion that I had value fuelled my resiliency. It was something I would not forget as an adult. Merlin was an important part of setting me on a path to success; he made a difference in my life.

I lived at home during university. I picked up a collection of summer jobs, normally connected to the university and continued to work for Merlin throughout the school year. I also continued to provide major support with the domestic and dog duties at home. Because I was earning outside income, my mother decided I should pay room and board. She was determined that I not get "a free ride." She would go on to tell the world that she worked hard to put me through university with her pet grooming service. What is sad is that I think she actually believed it to be true. If my father knew about this arrangement, he did not let on. Money became a serious issue for me. I certainly got none from my parents.

A friend was making a great income for a university student by waitressing. I decided to give it a go. If it went well, I could increase my income and reduce the number of hours I worked during the school term. In addition to working with Merlin, I had picked up a number of jobs with other professors, some of which included marking exams. I wanted to work a bit less for money and concentrate more on my studies. My parents hit the roof. Their response was loud and definite, "No daughter of ours is going to do a job like that!" Basically, if I waited tables to make money, I was acting like a whore and would need to move out.

I investigated a student loan. Parents were required to co-sign a loan if the applicant was under 21 years of age or had not lived away from home for two years or longer. I asked my parents to co-sign an application. They refused. They said, "No child of ours will go into debt to go to university." So I was left with the situation where I was paying room and board and was "not allowed" to work in more lucrative jobs if I was to remain at home with a roof over my head. It was yet again another illustration of my parents' extreme control issues. It was status quo until my 21st birthday on which day I submitted an application for a student loan. I received my loan at the end of November. I had my own place on December 1st. It is nice when plans come together.

At roughly the same time, my sister Charon ended her relationship with her husband and moved home. My mother had a slave back in the house. It was a testament to how damaged my sister was that she sought the sanctity of our parents' home. She also made the decision to move east with them when my father was transferred to the Toronto area. Immediately before my father was transferred, I had considered attending graduate school at McMaster University in Hamilton. Ironically, my future husband was doing graduate work at Mac at the time, and Charon would work there in the future. I rapidly changed my mind, and decided that my parents could leave the city. I would stay. I was due to convocate with my undergraduate degree that spring. My parents made it clear that they would not be coming back for the ceremony. To anyone who asked, I indicated that I did not give a damn. I decided I would not go to the ceremony. However, I did give a damn and regretted my decision not to attend my convocation. It slipped by, unmarked, just like any other day.

The scenario that had occurred between my mother and me was repeated with my sister. She lived at home and was instrumental in managing the house and its affairs in the hours when she was not working. My mother drank and became increasingly more paranoid. In due course, my sister, who was a warm and generous person, met a man. He built homes and was kind to her. My parents were dead set against the relationship. "He is not good enough for you." Charon ultimately married him. I am not sure how long it was that my mother refused to speak to my sister for defying her wishes. But, I believe Charon was comfortable with the silence.

On my own

I loved being a graduate student even more than being an undergraduate! I was fortunate enough to receive a major scholarship and the pressures of money lifted a bit.

My scholarship did not allow me to work outside the university setting, but I was able to make some extra money by grooming and showing dogs. I essentially began to run my own little business — one that lasted for three years. Just after I began graduate school, my sister Nancy and her husband Sam moved to the nearby city of Lethbridge. Nancy also showed terriers. We would meet up at dog shows throughout the province, share hotel rooms and a lot of laughs! With the exception of one disastrous Christmas when I went to my parents' place in Ontario, I spent all special occasions at Nancy's home in Lethbridge. I had roots and people close by who cared for me.

It was my sister and her husband who were the proud relatives in the audience when I convocated with my Master's degree. They, along with many other people from the dog game who were more aware of my struggles than I believed them to be, found it within their hearts to "find" me household essentials. My basement suite was outfitted with dishes, furniture and even food from people who cared for me. I was blessed. I was happy. I learned then as I know now that there are many good people in the world.

By the time I completed my graduate degree, I had publications in peer-reviewed journals, the first while I was still an undergraduate student. In my final three terms as an undergraduate, I took a number of graduate classes. By the time I entered my Master's program, I had most of the prerequisites for a graduate degree out of the way. My plans were to get my PhD. I looked into many programs, including some Ivy League Schools in the States.

As I was nearing the end of my Master's work, it was clear to me that I had neither the finances nor the emotional energy to begin a PhD program. I began to apply for jobs, and rapidly was offered a contract position in Edmonton with the Government of Alberta. I liked the idea of contract work because my plan, at that stage, was to work for a few years, bank some money and do my PhD. With my thesis 90% completed, I packed up my stuff and moved two and a half hours north to Edmonton. It took me another year to get the remaining 10% of my thesis done, and with the benefit of hindsight, I should never have made the move without it completed. It was hard to juggle full time work, complete my thesis, and manage the transition. And that transition was far harder than I thought it would be. Before the move and the job, I had been striving, fighting for everything. Now my existence had changed completely; I was effectively starting my life instead of preparing to live that life.

From a work perspective, I was coping well. But in moving to a new city, I had lost my community of supporters. I missed them terribly. Gradually, I gained friends and put down roots. My work for the Government was research and policy analysis in health manpower. I was good at research, and emerged to become a very competent policy analyst. I progressed within the government to more senior policy roles. About eight years after my move to Edmonton, I accepted a position as the Assistant Director of Research and Planning at the University of Alberta Hospital. The facility was one of the largest teaching hospitals in North America. I was in my element. By that point, I had clearly made the decision to abandon PhD studies. I loved health care too much and wanted to remain in the field.

One of my early responsibilities as Assistant Director was to help implement the newly approved heart transplant program. At first I was tentative in my new role. Working in government is very hierarchical, much like the military. There is a chain of command. Most government employees are used to every word in a document being scrutinized and edited at multiple levels of the hierarchy. I learned to love having greater independence on the job. Shortly after the heart transplant program was implemented, the hospital sought funding for a liver transplant program. I worked with the clinicians to prepare the submission to government. We were successful and the next year was spent in implementing the program.

When it was completed, I took on the role of administrator for all the transplant and renal programs. I was in my early thirties and had signing authority for a budget in excess of $12 million.

I began to write and present papers at conferences. I was an up and comer; my future plans were to be a senior executive in the health sector. I lived in a high rise apartment overlooking the river in the university district. I had come far from my basement suite struggling for money while fighting to complete my degree.

I remained very much aware that I had benefited from the generosity of others. In keeping with my moral code, I felt it important to give back. After I got established, I began volunteering. My first experience was as an in-house volunteer at Ronald McDonald house where families from outside Edmonton stayed while their children received care at the hospital where I worked. One holiday season I returned early from my sister's place in Lethbridge to be part of a group of volunteers who cooked New Year's supper for the families who could not get home for the holidays. Through connections with colleagues at work, I also began to volunteer with the Canadian Red Cross. When the tornado hit Edmonton in 1987 killing 27, I was the Chair of the Red Cross's Volunteer Resources Committee. The Red Cross was a major part of the tornado relief effort. With several others, I helped set up the Tornado Victims Assistance Centre in a high school close to where the tornado had been particularly deadly. My employer supported me by giving me time off with pay to complete this humanitarian work. The notion of volunteerism became part of the fabric of my existence. It even defined my social life.

I dated different men during this time and wanted very much to find a life partner. Some seemed intimidated by me and the positions I held. I was unwilling to compromise just for the sake of being with someone. I saw what that course of action had meant for my sister Charon. I felt it was better to be single than to be in a bad relationship. By this stage in my life I concluded I would never be married. However, fate would intervene. I met Paul.

My future husband

Paul says we would have met anyway. It was inevitable.
I was introduced to my future husband by one of my staff.

I was having a bad day, and Ingrid, the master conspirator, had a lunch date scheduled with Paul who had just moved to the city. She invited me to come along. I was resistant. Ingrid had been long going on about how the two of us should meet. That was enough to keep me away. I bent to pressure after the second conspirator, my assistant Mary, changed my schedule without my knowledge so I could go to lunch. I capitulated; I had to eat anyway. Paul and I rapidly entered into discussion. Poor Ingrid was like a spectator at a tennis match turning her head back and forth to follow the rapid fire dialogue between Paul and me.

I knew. I had seen the movies. I had read the books and was a non-believer. But on that day, I believed what I had not before. I knew that Paul was "the man." As I left the restaurant, I saw Paul walk to where I presume his car was parked. He limped. I thought he might have hurt his knee. But the limp did not go away, and Paul always walked very slowly. I was surprised to learn the reason.

Paul's family has roots in the Oro township area in the lake-district north of Toronto, a place where they vacationed every summer. Many of his relatives live there year round. It was in his Aunt's backyard, on the day before his family was to head back home from summer holidays, that Paul broke his back. He had constructed a tree fort, some 30 feet in the air, complete with a rope ladder. His father, upon seeing the fort, insisted Paul remove a tree stump present at its base. That saved his life, though I would question why any parent would allow their child to have a tree fort 30 feet in the air. When the rope ladder broke on that August day when Paul was 13, he was not impaled and killed by the tree stump. But he did break both his arms, bit through his tongue, and sustained a life altering spinal cord injury in the lower lumber region of his back.

Paul's father was a brilliant physician. First on scene, he administered emergency care. His actions likely prevented further injury to Paul's spinal cord. Paul would spend months hospitalized and strapped to a striker frame. One of his proud accomplishments was being able to eat, while upside down on the striker frame, one of his aunt's delectable but crumbly butter tarts!

Paul remained in hospital until just before Christmas. He speaks about learning to do wheelies on his wheelchair, and how once, in rolling, perhaps racing, down a ramp at the hospital, he plowed into a nurse holding a full tray of meds! Little pills went everywhere. He was in that nurse's bad-books for a time. He hid out in the hospital sun room until her shift was over! He was, after all, only 13 years old.

He ultimately regained some sensation on the inside of his legs, but was and still is unable to feel his feet and the outside of his legs. By the time he was discharged from hospital to outpatient care and rehabilitation, he was walking with the aid of a walker. He became a voracious reader and comic book collector during this period. He used to walk several blocks to the main street in his home in Stony Creek to buy a new comic book. Over the period of a year, Paul progressed from using a wheelchair, to a walker, to two crutches, then two canes, and finally one cane. After a year of trips for comic books, Paul had graduated to using only one cane. During one of these trips, a village barber, a person who did not know Paul but had watched his efforts, commented on how well he was doing in regaining his ability to walk. Several decades later Paul still remembers the barber's words of encouragement. He also marvels at the process by which children learn to walk so naturally, commenting on how hard it was for him the second time around.

Paul remains very humble about his significant rehabil-itation achievement. A few years after we were married, I bought us tickets to attend a speech by wheelchair athlete and advocate, Rick Hansen. The presentation was about setting and achieving goals. Rick spoke about his spinal cord injury and rehabilitation. Many of the experiences he shared that day were ones that Paul, too, had experienced. Unknown to me until then, I learned that both Rick and Paul had injured their spinal cords in the same spot. When the speech ended, Paul, somewhat emotionally commented on how strong Rick had been in recuperating from his injuries. Paul looked at me somewhat dumfounded when I replied that he, Paul, had showed just as much strength in regaining the use of his legs. He said, "But I just did what I had to do." I replied, "But what you did was impressive. Don't minimize the scope of your achievement."

When Paul arrived in Edmonton, he was in the process of rebuilding his life. He moved across the country to Vancouver to continue a relationship that ended three hours after he got off the plane. He stayed in Vancouver to work for a few years, but the time was not pleasant. Edmonton was a new start.

We took it slow and were companions for a long time before our relationship became serious. We maintained separate residences. I ultimately bought a house. When it became evident we were living together in two separate places, we decided it was time to accept the inevitable. I sold my house, and we bought a home together, got married a year later, and had Colin the next year.

Becoming parents

I joke and say that we got some of the order right! I also joke, somewhat seriously and say that we are geriatric parents. Certainly we were older than the other couples in the pre-natal class we attended before we had Colin.

When Paul and I got married, I was directing ambulatory care at a busy city hospital. Our marriage coincided with a significant downturn in the provincial economy that precipitated major changes in health care. I spent the year after our marriage in weekly meetings managing wholesale lay-offs. For the first time ever in my career, I hated what was happening at work.

The environment had morphed into a siege mentality rife with survivor sickness. I knew my job would also undergo significant change. When that time came, I made an important decision. I was offered the option to remain in a different job or take a package and leave. For many years, I had considered running my own business. I thought it was now time. I took the package.

My departure coincided with the beginning of the Lille-hammer Olympic Games. For the first time in my adult life,

I did nothing for a two week period except watch television and revel in the Olympics. I slept. I relaxed. I got pregnant!

We were simultaneously overjoyed and terrified. Pregnancy had eluded us for a year, and we were genuinely surprised when we learned I was pregnant. Initially, I felt fine. And then morning sickness hit and stayed, all day and night, for the first six months of my pregnancy. And every now and then, when I thought it had gone away, it came back.

We are the type of people who research everything. I approached my pregnancy in the same manner as I had tackled graduate school. I read books and articles and did my best to adhere to existing and emerging best practices for a pregnant woman. I ate healthy foods. The strongest beverage I drank was the occasional decaf coffee.

Our son arrived by c-section, over a week late, three days before Christmas. He was just shy of nine pounds and appeared to be a robust baby. We were, to put it mildly, ecstatic. Paul was punch drunk!

Because Colin was overdue, I was admitted to hospital to be induced late in the afternoon the day before he eventually made his appearance. By late evening, it was apparent that the baby was not coming immediately. Paul went home for some rest. When babies are involved, plans have a way of unraveling! By two in the morning, my contractions were a few minutes apart and the hospital called Paul to tell him to return. He drove my car, and, I suspect, screeched up to the entrance of the parking lot. During the day, the lot had a parking attendant. But in the middle of the night, entrance to the lot was guarded by an imposing yellow and black wooden parking arm. Paul looked around for a ticket dispenser or other way to get the arm to move up. He saw nothing. It was nighttime, cold, dark and his baby was about to be born. My car, old but loved, was a beater. So he gunned it. He drove through the gate leaving bright yellow paint marks on the roof of my car. The mangled parking arm lay on the ground by the car door pointing to my vehicle as the guilty culprit!

It was only a matter of time. The car was registered in my name. One of the hospital's security guards had the poor sense to walk into my room, mid contraction, and ask if I had wrecked the gate. The nurse pounced on him with the ferocity of a mother bear as Paul went out to confess to the deed. We suspected that others before us had driven through the gate. It was repaired while it was still dark. As we left the hospital, we stopped by the now intact parking gate to get a picture with our new baby boy!

We considered our son to be relatively healthy. But, a week after his birth, he needed chest x-rays to investigate respiratory problems. Looking back, we now realize that as a toddler and into his pre-school years, Colin suffered from continuous respiratory problems, ear infections and asthma. We are also aware that these health issues are strangely common among children with learning disabilities.

My mother

I was quick to embrace self employment soon after I left my hospital job. I loved being able to walk down the hall to my home office.

I gradually picked up contracts and by Colin's due date, was quite busy. My contracts were primarily in the field of health care, with a smattering of other jobs thrown in from time to time. Paul also entered the world of self-employment shortly before Colin was born. He too, worked from home, and this opportunity gave us both the chance to be with our new son and get to know him well.

When I was pregnant with Colin, I did take time to visit my parents. They had retired to Kelowna; my trip was deliberately short. My relationship with my parents had evolved, or devolved, to be fuelled by obligation rather than love. As an adult, I adopted the attitude that I should not expect anything from my parents. With this belief, I could only be pleased when they exceeded my expectations. Paul always said that he could tell when my mother and I had talked. Moodiness resulted.

One such phone call occurred a few months before I left the hospital job. I had appreciated that my position, along with the jobs of most of my colleagues, would change dramatically, and with that change, I would be eligible to receive an out-placement package. I had already made the decision to leave the hospital when that time came. However, there was still some grieving; the job I loved was evaporating. In the memorable phone call, my mother attacked me for my decision and the sadness I had expressed about the job situation. In her usual manner, she delivered a litany of negative comments about me. I stood my ground and replied, "You are my mother. I expect unconditional love and support from you. If you are not prepared to give me unconditional love and support, I don't want to speak to you." And we didn't for several months.

I was in a private room when Colin arrived. I had a phone. My parents did not call. They did not acknowledge the birth of their only grandchild. When I got home, there were flowers and cards of congratulations from other family and friends. There was nothing from my parents. We had been home from the hospital with Colin for about five days when the doorbell rang. A delivery person was swamped by a flower arrangement bundled up against the frigid December weather. I immediately assumed it would be flowers from my parents. They were from one of my clients, a thoughtful and appreciated gesture.

My mother did call about ten days after Colin was born. Nancy and Sam had wasted no time celebrating their status as a new auntie and uncle. They phoned me while I was still in hospital. What was interesting was that my mother and father had spent Christmas at Nancy's place that year, and chose not to join in on any conversations with me to celebrate the birth of their first grandchild. Nancy told me that our mother was frail and much older than her 65 years. Proud beyond belief with my new son, I said to Nancy, "Was she too frail to pick up the phone and call me? Is the phone that heavy?" Nancy really had no response. We both sighed, with many shared and unspoken thoughts about our mother. I knew why my mother had not called. Her expectations were that as the daughter, it was my obligation to call her. It was all about her. And was my father too frail? Certainly not.

Somehow, around the birth of our child, I had relaxed my rule about having no expectations about my parents. I thought a child might be cause for celebration. I was wrong.

My mother was hospitalized about 25 days after Colin was born. I am told that she did show Colin's baby pictures to the hospital staff. She died of a massive heart attack when Colin was four weeks old, her liver addled by years of drinking and non-prescription drug abuse, and her lungs hardened by emphysema from decades of smoking. There were about 20 people at her funeral, seven of whom included our small family of three, Nancy and Sam, Charon and my dad. It was a sad ending to a sad life.

Early words

Colin was physically precocious. He was walking at ten months. He was a curious and sunny child. He laughed easily and constantly. We anticipated that all would go according to plan!

He uttered his first words right on schedule. But, his speech was slow to evolve and we were slow to recognize the extent of his speech-language delays. Paul and I were often the only ones who could understand what Colin was saying. He was our first child. Our peer group did not have children his age. There were no grandmothers or extended family members around to point out to us what ultimately became obvious. Our wonderful son was slow in learning how to speak and when he was speaking, it was not clear.

We sought information and support. We have a wonderful family doctor, a man I knew from my days at the hospital. We asked him for advice. A practical person who often cites first principles, he said to us, "Let's first rule out possible hearing problems." We left with a referral for a hearing test at a pediatric audiology clinic and a suggestion that Colin have a speech-language assessment at our public health clinic. Public health units in our province provide many services from well baby clinics to immunizations. Speech-language assessment and therapy for youngsters are also provided, with all services being publicly insured and operated.

We appreciated the child friendly approach of the audiologist who conducted Colin's hearing test. I marveled at the play based strategies she used to assess his hearing. He came away from the testing thinking it was fun. We came away with the verdict that our son had excellent hearing. I would advise any parent with a child with speech and language problems to first get a hearing test. Rule out the obvious. If your doctor does not suggest a test, ask for a referral. Also place high on the to-do list, regular vision tests with a pediatric friendly optometrist.

The speech language assessment confirmed what we suspected. It revealed Colin had significant speech delays and that therapy was indicated. Colin was about two and a half. He went on a wait list for speech therapy.

We waited five months. Because we were willing to drive him to a public health unit anywhere in the city, we got in earlier than if we had decided to wait for a spot at the clinic near our home. His initial therapist was wonderful and Colin saw her once a week for ten weeks. He made progress. Then she went on maternity leave. There was a break of several months. Colin was then enrolled with another speech therapist for ten weeks who then also went on maternity leave. After a few months of waiting, we were able to get a spot for him with a speech therapist at our local health unit. Fortunately, it was close. Unfortunately, it was a disaster.

When it comes to health care, I have both high standards and high expectations. My biases and expectations emerge from having worked in the field. I don't believe they are un-realistic or unreasonable. I was not prepared for what I faced that day taking Colin for his first session with the new speech therapist.

In any pediatric clinical service, it is important to build trust with a child. It is perhaps even more important to build rapport and gain the trust of the parent. In my encounters with the health system with Colin, I was used to, in fact expected to be part of the process. In the previous speech therapy sessions, Paul or I, depending upon who was doing the driving that day, waited in a room apart from where Colin was getting his speech therapy but where he could see us. This is a very common approach in a pediatric environment. It is also common for clinicians, be they doctors, nurses, or therapists, to ask parents for insight into a child's condition and progress. Parents, after all, know their children better than others and can provide clinicians with valuable insight.

As I went to walk into the treatment area from the waiting room, the new therapist told me, "You are not allowed to come in with your son." In an even voice that denied the anger percolating beneath my manufactured calm demeanor, I replied, "That is unacceptable." She responded back to me,

"Children don't behave well when their parents are around."
My response, "I don't need to be in the same room but I
insist on being within his line of sight." Her response, "That
will be distracting. I don't allow parents in with me or around
me when I do therapy." My response, "I believe that violates
every sound principle of pediatric care. He is young and I am
insisting on observing the therapy." At that time, he was just
a little over three and a half years of age. I went on to say that
I would be happy to speak with her supervisor or the clinic
manager about the matter.

   I did observe the therapy. She made no effort to establish
rapport with Colin or engage in age appropriate interactions.
She was task oriented to the point of being unfeeling and
robotic. She continued to treat me with disdain.

   Sadly, in the journey of advocacy for our son, now approaching 16 years, Paul and I have been regarded by many
different professionals as stupid, ignorant, or irresponsible.
Other parents of children with exceptional needs have told me
that they too, have been judged this way. It is tough to say what
fuels this all too prevalent attitude. Some people have shared
with me a phrase used out of earshot to describe people like
me — a parent of a child with exceptional learning needs. The
phrase is something along the line, "Special-ed kids, special-ed
parents." It is meant to be insulting. I have encountered people
who definitely adhere to this negative motto. Their views,
however, have been offset by many wonderful and caring
professionals. But, this was the first time I had been evaluated

in a negative manner because of the attributes of my son.
I was not impressed.

After the session, it took very little time for me to identify
the management chain of command for the therapist. I placed
a call to complain. I described what happened. I also let it slip
that I thought the Director would want to have this input, as
when I had held senior positions in the hospital sector, I appreciated feedback so as to enable positive changes to take place.
Throughout this exchange, I adhered to a basic principle —
I did not attack the therapist. I did not make it personal. What
I did do was raise my concerns about the therapist's behavior
and the practices I witnessed. To me, this distinction is subtle
but important. I am not suggesting professionals should not be
accountable for their actions. I think exactly the opposite. But
actions and words on any given day do not define a person's
existence.

My call made a difference. There was a definite détente
in subsequent sessions. But we had no faith or trust. Our
relationship with this care provider had been irrevocably
damaged from the initial meeting. It deteriorated even further
when she interpreted test results to mean Colin was unintel-
ligent. I challenged her interpretation of the numbers. She
was resolute. We knew better.

We immediately sought the services of a private speech
therapist. I have no idea how we ultimately linked up with
Donna, but luck was shining down upon us that day! She was
a busy speech therapist in private practice. In a curious twist

of fate, I learned she was the daughter of good friends of my sister, Charon. Donna's parents lived in Ontario, down the street from Charon, and were very much like her surrogate parents.

Instead of once a week, Colin now had speech therapy two to three times a week. Progress, at least from our perspective, was brisk. Donna taught Colin how to identify words, speak in sentences, and understand what is innate in most people — the basic premises of grammar, verb conjugation, and concepts like singular and plural. He began to speak more. As that happened, we began to understand Donna's concern about his speech. We were able to hear quite clearly the speech patterns commonly known as stuttering.

Bumpy speaking

Bumpy speaking is a child friendly and very clear way to describe stuttering. Bumpy is also a suitable description of a family's journey when they have a child with exceptional needs — certainly it can be used to describe ours.

Donna connected us with ISTAR (Institute for Stuttering Treatment and Research) affiliated with the University of Alberta in Edmonton. Approaching five years of age, Colin began intense therapy at ISTAR. Colin's level of stuttering was rated moderate. I have since forgotten what distinguishes a person with mild, moderate or severe levels of stuttering, but do recall that before treatment, Colin would repeat a sound at the beginning of a word about five times and do this with several words during one minute of speech to a total of about 60 repetitions per minute.

Colin's treatment for stuttering lasted about a year. For the first six months, Colin went to ISTAR three times per week. A home program was also part of the treatment plan. As the year progressed, the number of visits per week was reduced. By the end of the year, Colin was no longer a bumpy speaker.

We occasionally note hesitations and lack of fluency in his speech, but only a very knowledgeable person would be able to discern that Colin had previously been affected by stuttering. His treatment was an amazing success.

We had public reinforcement of its success the spring after Colin started ISTAR. On a lovely Saturday, our family went to a penny arcade that was being held at an historic home on the University of Alberta campus. There was old fashioned candy, sack races and various other activities designed to entertain young children. A local television station was on site inter-viewing children about what they were doing, Colin among them. He took great pride in explaining a game he had played. Many kids were interviewed, and we had no expectations that his spot would be the one to play at supper on television that night. But Colin was the featured child. The news host, at the end of the segment, exclaimed, "How cute." And he was, complete with speech that was not at all bumpy!

Ranting about waiting to fail

With the benefit of some emotional distance, it is possible to look back and analyze our initial encounters "with the system," in this case speech therapy services.

It was in this early stage of our son's life that we heard for the first through four hundredth time, "Children develop differently. Don't be alarmed. Let's just wait and see." In most instances, this comment is intended to comfort worried parents. But, now, when I hear that phrase, it effectively elevates my blood pressure. What begins as an anxiety reducing platitude for parents of toddler and pre-school children evolves into the all too common and universally decried *"wait to fail"* mentality that permeates our school systems.

If there ever was a truism in health care and rehabilitation, it is "earlier is better." Children move through developmental stages at warp speed, with brains characterized by high levels of plasticity and developmental capacity. While brain plasticity and the ability to create new neuro-pathways continue into old age, the brain of a child is particularly receptive to speech-language and physio-motor therapies that enhances learning.

But we fail to capitalize on this reality when we say, "Let's just wait and see."

It is time for a new motto. Yes, each child is unique. But instead of saying, "Let's wait and see," perhaps we could say, "Let's check and be sure. Let's formulate and implement a plan to address your child's concerns, and evaluate whether that plan is making a difference in the next two to three months...."

Action rather than inattention is required, and it is needed at the earliest possible stages in a child's life. Let's capitalize on the miracle of those wonderful developing brains and the ability to prevent problems early rather than try to remediate them later. Let's obliterate this wait to fail mentality. It destroys lives.

Another observation I can make pertains to the complete lack of an early warning system. We have the information and expertise from research based practices to implement early therapy and supports. With the benefit of knowledge about learning disabilities, we were able to look back and note that Colin had exhibited a number of risk factors at a very early age. Chief was speech and language delays. How valuable it might have been for the speech language therapists in our lives to have said, "Speech language delays can be a risk factor for learning disabilities. You may want to monitor your child's progress when he starts school to see if this is the case. Learning disabilities are...." I guess an even more pertinent question might be whether speech therapists are aware that the children they treat are at high risk for learning disabilities.

At no time did any professional during Colin's pre-school

years pass this little and highly important tidbit of information to us. All things considered, I wish we would have been given this information. I would have preferred to have been prepared than to have missed the signs, and failed to get support at the earliest possible stage. And that is exactly what happened.

Matters of money and work

When we decided to hire a private speech therapist for Colin, we began a financial journey that paralleled our advocacy journey. It is expensive to have a child with exceptional needs, even in the land of socialized medicine. It is also not too compatible with working nine to five.

When Colin was two and a half, we were ecstatic over the arrival of his brother Kyle. We became a family of four. Like Colin, both Paul and I had the chance to spend a great deal of time with Kyle because we were self-employed. It was an opportunity we valued so highly.

When Kyle was still in diapers, we decided that one of us needed to get a regular job. A significant downside to being self-employed is the lack of medical benefits. While it is possible to purchase medical plans as a self employed person, the cost of these programs can be prohibitive. Though he enjoyed self-employment, Paul obtained a salaried position at the University of Alberta managing Information Technology in one of the Faculties. He held or more accurately tolerated the position for four years. The decision to return to an employment situation was to provide stability for our family.

We paid out of pocket for the expensive third-generation antibiotics that normally accompanied the frequent trips we made to the hospital for Colin's serious ear infections. We also paid privately for Colin's speech therapy services and the other medical services and prescriptions any of us needed. With a second child, medical and dental benefits were becoming more important considerations in our life.

There was some irony that the University benefit plan did not cover the cost of services provided by ISTAR — one of its high profile and internationally known programs. Colin accessed those services while Paul was still a faculty member. We were able to set aside the money for the treatment. We were fortunate; not all families with children with severe speech issues have those resources. Private speech therapy and ISTAR signified the beginning of our realization of just how expensive it is to provide a range of supports for children with exceptional needs.

While various company plans cover some expenses, they do not cover all, and many families either suffer significant financial hardship or forego the services. Some plans require authorization in advance in order to insure a service. It may be possible, if both parents are working, to coordinate benefits from two plans for services like psycho-educational assessments, speech therapy, counseling, assistive technology assessments, etc. Often, the professionals involved in providing these services will be able to offer advice on the best strategies for coordinating benefits between two insurance plans.

Employment benefits may be theoretical if it is impossible to keep a job because of the demands of managing services for children with exceptional needs. Taking children to various appointments during the day, often multiple times a week, is not compatible with working a regular nine to five job. Self-employment provided Paul and me with the flexibility we needed to manage Colin's various appointments. Looking back, I do not believe we would have been able to handle those demands if one of us had not been self-employed. I had the ability to juggle my schedule. With Paul's support, I could shift my work to the evening on those days when Colin had daytime appointments and I had work deadlines. I also became the queen of early morning work. I began my day at 5:00 am. I would awaken, tend to our new baby, and then work quietly until the day started getting busy again at 8:00 am. It worked for us.

Interviewing principals
In search of a school

It is emotionally difficult to send your child off to kinder-garten when he or she is "normal" — whatever that might be. But, a parent's anxiety can rise to stratospheric levels when their child has some exceptional needs.

Paul and I were both excited and frightened for Colin to begin kindergarten. He was a veritable sponge for information. His favorite show was the *Magic School Bus*. Fortunately, it was also a show we enjoyed watching with him! We read books to both Colin and Kyle on a regular basis. We played alphabet games. We had dreams and aspirations for both our sons that envisioned them as happy, healthy and self actualized adults. We still have those dreams but we know Colin may have a harder time than others in attaining this state.

Though Colin's stuttering had responded very well to therapy, we worried he would be the target of school yard bullies because of his speech issues. We wanted to do everything we could to ensure his school experience was one where he would be safe and happy. We wanted a place where he could maximize his educational potential. At this stage, we had no idea he had learning disabilities or attention issues, though looking back, both were clearly evident. We just did not know the signs.

We began to do research. We identified schools within a two kilometer radius of our home and the day care our children now attended. The public school systems in our city have open boundaries. While each school has an obligation to accept children in their catchment area, families have the option of selecting schools outside their community. These schools typically have programs of choice or specific instruc-tional philosophies that appeal to the needs or interest of a family. Open boundaries have good and bad consequences, but we embraced the benefit of choice in order to address Colin's particular needs.

I was raised in a Roman Catholic family. For that reason, our options included both public and Catholic school systems. We asked neighborhood children about their experiences at schools in our community. Our next door neighbor worked as a social worker in our sector of the city. She had definite ideas about schools and we considered her input seriously.

A client with a background in education provided highly valued advice. He said, "Consider the leadership of the school." The premise was that the environment and quality of a school flows from the principal. Having now experienced ten years of school life through our children, we believe this to be abso-lutely true.

We started immediately after Christmas arranging appoint-ments with principals on our short list of schools. The entire process was highly illuminating. We immediately struck one school from the list because, as we were advised after repeated requests for a meeting, "The principal does not DO interviews with parents!"

One interview was particularly memorable. Paul and I were waiting for an early morning appointment with a principal in a school close to our home. A young boy walked up to the school secretary. The secretary did not speak to the boy but upon seeing him, wheeled over to a file cabinet drawer and removed a pill from a container. She gave him the pill that he took without water. She wheeled back to her work and the boy walked away. The administration of medication had been completed without the adults at the school speaking to this boy or showing that they cared in any way at all. Paul and I exchanged looks that signaled how appalled we both were with what we had witnessed.

Quickly afterwards, we were ushered into the principal's office. After the routine preamble, we described Colin's speech issues. We asked the principal how we could work in partnership with the school to address our son's unique needs. She told us about a district reading program, called Balanced Literacy, that the school offered. I repeated the question about our son's needs. I was then reprimanded and told she had answered my question. Our question had not been addressed. Instead, we had been chastised like little children who had done something wrong. We could only imagine what it would be like to be a child with exceptional learning needs in that school. Actually, I could not imagine being any child in that school!

The next interview resulted in us striking yet another school off our list. Paul could not attend, and I went solo. I began with the same question we had asked at the previous school, "How could we work in partnership with the school to address Colin's unique needs?" The principal responded by making reference to our son's learning disability. I corrected him. I indicated that Colin had speech issues and not a learning disability. He responded by saying that the first thing he would do would be to get me over my concerns about labeling!

The irony was that our son did have a learning disability — something we would learn four years later. But stuttering is not a learning disability. It is wrong to make assumptions. It is worse to batter a concerned parent. If I was to be generous, I might assume the principal concluded there was a risk of a learning disability based on Colin's speech issues. If this was the case, the interaction with me might have been much more productive if he had said that speech issues are often associated with learning disabilities, and that it would be wise for all of us to monitor Colin's progress as a precautionary measure.

In total, five schools were on our "short list." Ultimately, two landed in the top spot based on the strength of the interviews with the principals. We eliminated the "second" place school because the principal would likely be leaving within the year, consistent with the district practice of limiting a principal's tenure in one spot to about six years. Fortunately, we were able to enroll our son in a kindergarten program with a superb teacher. Unfortunately, we had to pull him from that same school in the early weeks of grade one.

If our experience is any indication, principals need to be part psychologist or at least adept at reading both the substance and context of a situation. I have met some principals who have been extraordinary in communicating with parents and making every child welcome in a school. But, the opposite also occurs. I have since heard from parents of children with exceptional learning needs that they have been told bluntly by school principals that a school may not be the best "fit" for their child... even though it is the school the child's siblings attend. I do not believe that we were deliberately driven away by some of the principals we interviewed in our quest to find the right school for Colin. But, we know there is huge variation in the willingness of some schools to embrace and support students with exceptional learning needs. Our family's early experience spotlights the frustration of families who simply want to ensure that their child with exceptional needs is placed in an environment where they can be happy, safe, and maximize their educational potential.

Kindergarten and acts of kindness

We have many pictures of that first day! We were so proud. Our son was starting kindergarten. He was excited but so were we!

We had done our homework and were satisfied with our choice of schools. My husband and I worked as partners to support Colin's needs. We both went to open houses, the meet the teacher night, and all the parent-teacher interviews. Colin's kindergarten teacher, Alison, was highly familiar with stuttering and the treatment protocol at ISTAR. Fortunately, by the time Colin began kindergarten, the repetitive speech, characteristic of stuttering, was infrequent. We were so pleased.

Because of Colin's speech delays and stuttering, we were not in a hurry, as the expression goes, to get into trouble. His birthday was in late December. We decided to have him enter kindergarten when he was five turning six rather than four turning five years of age. The latter would result in him being one of the youngest students in the class and the former among the oldest.

Our initial reason for delaying the start of kindergarten was to provide him with time to benefit from speech therapy at

ISTAR. But there were other collateral benefits of this decision, many of which we were not initially aware. Many educators and mental health professionals express the view that youth who are slightly older than the average age of their cohort are better able to withstand peer pressure when they are in junior high. Of course, their age in junior high, relative to their peer group, is dependent upon the age they start kindergarten. Another factor, one unknown to us at the time, is that children with learning disabilities and attention disorders tend to be more immature than their peers on a social and emotional level. Some estimates place the difference between their chronological and emotional age at two to three years.

Colin's kindergarten experience was very successful. His teacher, Alison, is an engaging, caring and gifted educator. Because Colin had been at day care, he had no difficulties socializing with other students and getting used to the school routine. He was and remains a person that respects rules and does not like getting into trouble; his moral compass is well developed. That motivation truly drove him to try to do his best.

One of the real assets of Colin's kindergarten experience was how Alison introduced the class to literacy. She used a number of strategies, one of which was American Sign Language (ASL). Signing was popular and appealed to the different learning preferences of students. A decade later, many of her students, including Colin, still remember some rudimentary signing.

A few years after Colin was in her class, Alison went on to complete a Master's degree. She explored several strategies for introducing language to students including visual, auditory and kinesthetic cues. Using multiple strategies capitalizes on the different ways every unique brain "processes" language. It is also fun as there is variety in the way a subject is presented. This engages students and supports learning.

During the parent conferences that accompanied the second report card, we asked Alison if she noticed Colin having problems grasping the basic concepts of reading and writing. Because of Colin's excellent ability to retain verbal information, we were surprised and a bit worried about how long it was taking him to gain the technical skills associated with reading and writing. The answer was that he was doing fine in comparison to his peer group but that it was too soon to tell if he had any learning challenges.

We now know that extensive effort to gain mastery of a subject area, particularly when it is widely accepted that a person has average to above average intelligence or cognitive ability, is symptomatic of learning disabilities. In retrospect, Colin's interest in school, desire to do well, and failure to rapidly gain mastery of reading and writing, was compelling evidence of his learning disabilities. He was one of the older children in the class. And, I could not help comparing his progress to mine. I was both reading and writing before I began school, thanks to my "teacher," my sister Nancy.

Interestingly, a chance encounter with Alison four years later resulted in a different answer to our question about his progress after his second report card. She was aware Colin had been diagnosed with learning disabilities. She told me that if she had had the benefit of the knowledge she gained while completing her Master's degree, she likely would have considered the possibility that Colin had learning disabilities when he was still in kindergarten. Her comments somehow validated our initial parental concerns. Her willingness to share this with me spoke to her character.

During this same conversation, she also told me that she had used Colin as an example in one of her graduate seminars. I immediately thought it had to do with his learning disabilities. But, she went on to say that it was to illustrate kindness. I obviously had a puzzled expression on my face. Seeing that, she quickly realized she had never told us this story. Knowing Colin had an incredible talent for losing mittens, I always put a spare pair in his backpack. In the line up to go out for recess on a very cold Edmonton day, Colin noticed that one of his classmates had no mittens. Without saying a word, he went to his backpack, pulled out the spare pair of mittens, and then gave them to his classmate. This was done in a quiet manner, and Colin was unaware that the entire exchange was being witnessed — at a distance, by Alison. He proceeded to explain to the little girl that his mother always packed an extra pair of mittens, and that she should take them. Alison told me how impressed she had been at the time with his generosity and used the story about his gift to illustrate kindness in children. I left the conversation with such a warm feeling and pride in our son, and respect for this amazing teacher.

The bully, the bystanders and all the things you did wrong today

We were full of hope. We had researched the school. Our selection was based on the premise that Colin and then Kyle would receive all seven years of elementary education at this school.

Colin's kindergarten experience had been outstanding. We expected grade one to go the same way. But, it did not. There were two factors that drove us away from our carefully selected school...his actual experience in the grade one classroom and a breakout of bullying that affected both the school and the day care he attended.

The bullying started at the daycare over the summer months. Like a bad virus, it spread across the parking lot to infect Colin's school. A child, about four years older than Colin and significantly bigger and heavier, began to bully several children at the day care. Colin became one of his favorite targets.

The daycare, previously wonderful, had new leadership and handled the situation in a terrible manner. Bullying issues must be addressed quickly and with compassion for the benefit of all children — the bullied, the bully, and all the bystanders or witnesses. Unfortunately, the daycare management let the situation fester and minimized the seriousness of the physical and mental abuse that the bully was ministering to younger and more vulnerable children. Ultimately, the situation exploded with several parents pulling their children and placing them in other facilities.

As one of the bully's favorite targets, Colin was pushed on stairs, had his shoes stolen and buried in the playground, was shoved on playground equipment in a very unsafe manner, and had his personal belongings thrown back and forth over his head by the bully and other children the bully conscripted. These are the types of incidents we found out about — there were undoubtedly more. We heard from one parent that the bully had put their son in a chokehold around the neck midway up a concrete set of stairs.

In order to "make the children get along," the day care management insisted Colin play with the bully. During one of these command performances, Colin was on a teeter totter with the bully. Colin jumped off without warning, resulting in the bully coming down hard on his butt. Our son got into trouble for not "playing nice." It was one of those no win situations as the behavior of the bully seemed to go unchecked in the view of many protesting parents. When school started, the bully was in a classroom a few doors down from Colin. He used the same door to get in and out of the school, and transferred his bullying ways to the school playground. Colin felt terrorized.

Then there was the actual grade one class. On the first day of school, Paul and other parents of grade one students were invited to stay in the class for the first period. There were about 25 students in the class and the teacher had each one remain seated and tell everyone about themselves and their family. This occurred for about 90 minutes without breaks until the first recess. Some children were terrified to speak and others were so bored with the proceedings that they fussed and fidgeted in their chairs. Many of the parents also fussed and fidgeted, Paul among them. The reason for the discussion was laudable — to enable students to get to know each other. But in an early elementary grade, the wisdom of having children sit still at a desk for a 90 minute stretch was questionable.

Colin's grade one teacher was regarded by the parent community as a tough disciplinarian. She expected students to sit quietly at their desks, listen, and work. She appeared autocratic but was able to get results from a number of students. Her style, however, was horrific for Colin and such a contrast from his engaging and kind kindergarten teacher. Colin had trouble sitting still for extended periods of time. He had trouble listening without a break. He had trouble meeting her expectations.

As September marched on, the situation deteriorated. A strategy the teacher used each time Colin had trouble completing work or sitting still was to pull his desk so he was separate from all the other children. In a classroom with desks organized with military precision row upon row, Colin's was frequently off to the side. He was different and that difference was being reinforced.

The combination of being identified as different and fears about being bullied resulted in Colin hating grade one by mid September. We met with the teacher to discuss how to turn the situation around. We discussed the practice of pulling Colin's desk off to the side. We discussed how the school was handling the bullying issue. We shared with the school ISTAR resources on the prevention of teasing and bullying. We tried to give back. Our goal was to make grade one a better place for our child and all the other students.

One outcome of that meeting was the conclusion that home and school communication needed to improve. We procured a small notebook for the teacher to use to record key messages for us about Colin's day. In the next three weeks, it contained a litany of all the things he had done wrong. Not once were any positives recorded — no praise, no encour- agement, no focus on our son's strengths. And the bullying continued. We were told that after we left the school, a child was duct taped to a post by the bully. Somehow, that got everyone's attention.

We were confused. We realized that Colin, like all children, was not perfect. We knew he was not the first child to have trouble listening for extended periods of time in class. But we did know that Colin was a very bright, good and kind person. We were not trained as teachers, and wanted to place our trust in professional educators. Yet we were certain that the way he was being taught was not meeting his needs. Did that make our son bad? No! We believe his teacher and the school failed him. It was up to the professionals, i.e., the teachers, to use their repertoire of skills to ascertain how our child learned and to try to accommodate his needs. Pushing him to the side of the class and recording all his failings without consideration of his strengths was simply unacceptable. It marginalized him. He deserved better...he deserved to have his educational potential maximized, *just like all the other children in his class.*

We were now very worried. If the first few weeks of grade one were a predictor of the future, we were concerned Colin would experience significant stress and mental health issues as a direct consequence of his struggles in elementary school. We were certainly concerned he would lose his love of learning.

We put some short-term measures in place to support him until we figured out what to do. Paul dropped him off immediately before school started so he did not need to deal with the bully on the school playground. I waited for him at school dismissal time. This meant he would not have to go to after school care to be bullied. We completely reorganized our family and business schedules. In the meantime, I started making phone calls to look for an alternative.

Situations change. We learned so many times as parents that what might be great at one time can change in a heart-beat. I believe, quite strongly, that it is our job as parents and the birthright of our children, to watch out for their needs. Constant vigilance is required. The situation changed at the daycare. As loyal clients for a number of years, the decision to part ways was difficult. But, it was absolutely something we had to do. The situation also changed at the school. What was once good deteriorated. As parents, we tried to work within the system. We spoke to Colin's teacher. We met with the principal. We focused on the situation. We did not make it personal. We respectfully sought change.

We believe the school failed Colin miserably in grade one. It failed to do anything practical to make our child, and others, safe from bullying. And, while our son's grade one teacher clearly viewed Colin as having some learning challenges, she did not appear to do anything to address his needs. The situation became personalized with the focus on Colin's weaknesses. Colin's struggles were defined as the problem rather than a symptom of his learning issues. As an obviously smart child with a track record of trying to "be good and obey the rules," we believe it would have been important for the education professionals in his life to ask the important question, "What is going on?"

On the move
A new school and a new outlook

The search was on to look for a new school for Colin. Unlike before, our parameters for a new school were not confined to our neighborhood. Though distance was a consideration, the need to remain in our community was not.

In a two week period, I lost count of the number of people with whom I spoke. I connected with many caring individuals. Their willingness to give me time and the benefit of their experience was very much appreciated. Though these telephone calls blurred, one into the other, I do remember one call vividly. A woman, commenting on a possible school option for Colin said she thought it would be a place where he would be "safe." Unexpectedly, I became quite emotional.

Over the past several years, I have spoken to many parents of children with exceptional needs. A number of them have become quite emotional, breaking out in tears in the midst of our conversation. Inevitably, these parents apologize for crying. I tell them not to apologize, that there is no need to do so, and that I understand. I truly do. I have been there, not once, but many times.

It seemed like the goals for Colin had shifted from maximizing his educational potential to the more basic need of keeping him safe. We wanted him to feel like he could belong, and play and interact with other children without the fear of being bullied. And along the way, we wanted him to be educated too. But, somehow that primary goal was now taking a second place. For a couple that placed as much value as we did on education, things were a bit mixed up.

I found a website for an alternative program within Edmonton Public Schools. It focused on project based learning to explore language, math, science, art and other areas of the curriculum. It was a style of learning Paul and I instinctively liked. We were also pleased with the program's emphasis on citizenship and community. The program was located in Strathearn School in a mature neighborhood, similarly named, about a twenty minute drive from our home. The school was involved in a small class size initiative and had a full day kindergarten. With Kyle's needs to consider, the full day kindergarten was particularly appealing. It also had a very popular after school care program located right in the school. We were optimistic that the program and the school might be a good fit for our family. We phoned and asked if we could see the program in action. The teacher immediately invited us to come and visit. We asked what time would be good. She replied, "Anytime. Parents are always welcome in my classroom." She also encouraged us to bring Colin along for the visit.

A few days before Halloween we set off to see the school. Colin was warmly greeted by both the teacher and the students of the grade one to three split class. The room was colorful — in fact it was a feast for the eyes. There were dioramas, books, posters, aquariums, puppet theaters, rocks, plants, and various other items that could be used to help illustrate lessons. Different types of work stations were situated throughout the room; they complemented regular student desks located in the centre of the class. This type of room layout was only possible in a big classroom — typical of those in schools built in the post war baby boom. Strathearn School was of that vintage.

All the students, with our son, formed a circle in an open carpeted area. Colin was introduced and welcomed. The students took turns telling him a bit about each other and used the opportunity to ask him questions. However, unlike the experience on his first day of grade one, this introduction was expedient and child friendly. About half way through this process, Colin politely excused himself and walked over to where we were sitting at the back of the room. He told us he wanted to stay at this school, and never go back to the other school. We told him we were thinking seriously about him staying.

He was invited to participate in a class play that was being organized based on a Halloween story that had been read in class. It was one that was familiar to Colin — something we had read with him. He enthusiastically took part. Once again, midway through the preparations, he excused himself and came to us pleading to stay at this new school. We stayed for the entire day. We stayed for the remainder of the year. Our family stayed until the school board voted to close the school.

We called his existing school and told the administration Colin would not be returning. We were not asked why. Arrangements were made to pick up his things. We moved on.

We did not live in Strathearn's designated catchment area. However, the principal was willing to accept Colin eight weeks into the term. We learned later how unusual and generous a gesture this was. While schools in our city have an obligation to accept students from their designated communities after the beginning of the term, principals have flexibility to deny entrance to children from outside their catchment areas. Within our school district, a school's budget, or more specifically its revenues, is based on the number of children enrolled on September 30th. We missed that deadline by almost four weeks and the school did not benefit financially from Colin being enrolled.

Almost overnight, Colin regained his love of school. The environment was safe. The school was a joint elementary and junior high and had a wonderful sense of community. Parents were warmly welcomed and valued in the classroom. It was not uncommon for parents with specialized knowledge to be a guest speaker in any of the kindergarten to grade nine classes. The respect for the parent community was a major factor in generating a love for the school — something that would be

highly evident four years later when the community fought
furiously to keep Strathearn from being closed.

In Colin's class, time was set aside every morning for
parents to come in until about 9:00 am to read with their
children. It was not unusual for several students to be gath-
ered around a parent reading a book aloud. Siblings were also
welcomed, and Kyle, two and a half years younger than Colin,
was a frequent visitor. Socially, Colin thrived. But despite this
warm and enriched environment, he continued to struggle
to gain the technical skills necessary to read and write.

Emerging awareness of our son as a struggling reader

Colin was happy in his new grade one class. He was safe. There was no bully around the corner. He was now formally enrolled in the new school. Things started to unravel in the second term, but we had three blissful months where everything seemed fine.

Yet, I had a sense that something was "off" with the way he was learning to read. Even with an intensive focus on reading, Colin could not read simple words or identify successfully, basic letter sounds. It was impossible for him to sound out a word. He protested strongly if we asked him to try to read a story to us though he loved reading times and always begged for bedtime stories.

Colin continued with regular lessons that were part of the grade one curriculum. This included the common practice of writing letters in upper and lower case on work sheets. He struggled. We were encouraged to purchase paper designed for children learning to print. These sheets had dotted lines between two solid lines to provide guides for the new writer to gauge the size of upper and lower case letters. Being somewhat comfortable with the computer, I made my own for Colin, complete with cool clip art at the top or bottom of the page. Printed on colored paper, Colin had the coolest paper in the class. It was soon copied!

Instinctively, I kept thinking Colin needed to go back to the basics. My instinct was not that far off. I thought he was failing to gain an understanding of the basic elements of reading and writing... specifically, letters and the sounds they made. I thought we might be able to help him by purchasing some instruction manuals and giving him additional support outside school.

With the burgeoning home school movement, there are many curriculum based resources available for purchase. I began to peruse resources at local book stores. I thought I could try to reintroduce Colin to the basics. During this quest, I found a book that would significantly enhance my understanding of Colin's challenges. Its title initially caught my attention: *Parenting a Struggling Reader: A Guide to Diagnosing and Finding Help for Your Child's Reading Difficulties* by Susan L. Hall and Louisa C. Moats. It would be the first of many resources I would study in my quest to learn more about reading problems.

I was intrigued by the concept of phonemic awareness and how it impacts language instruction, something Hall and Moats described in their book. There are 44 sounds or phonemes that make up the English language. It is phonemes that children sound out when learning how to read. Phonemic awareness refers to the ability to distinguish and manipulate these sound bites; it is an essential skill set for reading and writing. Colin clearly had limited ability to distinguish the sounds in the English language. As I read the book, it became very evident to me that Colin had poor phonemic awareness! I felt that I had identified his major stumbling block in acquiring the technical skills necessary to read and write.

The book also provided an overview of strategies used by educators to teach early literacy. Some children are taught to read and write with specific instruction in phonetics. This approach places emphasis on how to decode or distinguish phonemes and letter sounds. It is part of creating a sound — symbol connection, the symbol being the letters on the page that make up a part of a word.

At the other end of the continuum is the whole language approach. It is based on the principle that children learn to read and write as naturally as they learn to talk. Because children can talk, the theory is that they can automatically learn to read — that this skill is innate. The practical implication is that children can learn to read by being exposed to literature. The whole language approach places little or no emphasis on phonetics.

And, of course, there is a middle ground where reading and writing instruction includes elements of both phonics and whole language approaches. It is often called a balanced approach or balanced literacy. To confuse matters, balanced literacy may also be used to describe a specific literacy program. There is, for example, a Balanced Literacy program used in many schools, including some within our public school district.

There is debate amongst the education community about language education. Phonics, or teaching reading by associating letters with their sounds (a sound symbol connection), is considered by some to be an unpopular and tedious way to teach language. A significant proportion of teacher training programs do not provide instruction on how to teach language using phonics. This is unfortunate because it is critical that children with poor phonemic awareness be conversant with phonics in order to learn to read and write.

The Hall and Moats book was critical for me for a number of reasons. It clearly demonstrated that Colin was not unique or unusual; there was a definite reason for his struggles. And more profoundly, I realized that in his new enriched learning environment, Colin was being taught to read using a whole language approach! He was failing miserably because he had poor phonemic awareness. He had exhibited evidence of his poor phonemic awareness in kindergarten. However, his kindergarten teacher's approach to early literacy had included instruction on the sound bites in the English language. But now he was missing the very thing he needed to successfully learn how to read and write.

Not every professional is always professional

*I was only beginning to scratch the surface of what could
be impacting Colin's ability to learn to read and write.
I knew we needed more information.*

The Hall and Moats book, *How to Parent a Struggling Reader*,
clearly described learning disabilities. But somehow, I failed to
identify Colin as being at risk for learning disabilities. I focused
on his poor phonemic awareness. I did not connect the dots.

Poor phonemic awareness is one of the defining characteristics of people with the reading disability also known as dyslexia.
There are many different types of learning disabilities, but the
most common, at about 80%, is reading disabilities.

The awareness that Colin had a learning disability or disabilities would come later. But at that time, Paul and I were in
denial. I reasoned that none of his teachers had ever suggested
he had a learning disability. I mistakenly thought that if learning
disabilities were suspected, then this concern would have been
raised by one of the professional educators in Colin's life. This
was a logical but unwise assumption. Unfortunately, teachers, as
a group, have limited understanding about learning disabilities.

And it is not their fault.

Most teachers are generally not provided with pre-service education on the signs and symptoms of learning disabilities. In many teacher education programs, instruction on special education is optional. The result — it is entirely possible to graduate without having learned how to identify learning disabilities or how to teach students affected by learning disabilities. This is a critical deficiency when we consider that a conservative incidence of learning disabilities is one out of every ten people.

I knew nothing about learning disabilities at this stage of our family's journey. This, in itself, was telling. I considered myself well versed on a number of health and social issues. I had worked my entire career in health care. I had done extensive consulting work in children's mental health and at risk youth. My preconceived notions about learning disabilities were incorrect. I thought people with learning disabilities could not learn easily and were not smart. Our son was more than capable of learning. He was smart. Clearly, I needed to dismantle some of my preconceived ideas.

After Christmas during grade one, we decided to try to gain a better understanding about the factors affecting Colin's learning. We sought advice from our family doctor. He referred us to a psychologist to get Colin a psycho-educational assessment. We wanted to pursue this option privately. We were concerned about labeling Colin. We harbored a fear that an assessment conducted through the school system would limit his educational options if the results turned out to be "bad." As advocates for our son, we were obsessed with maintaining some control. But on a practical level, we had absolutely no idea that a psycho-educational assessment could be provided by our school district. We did not know what to expect from the system or what the system was obligated to provide.

We made the appointment. On one of the coldest days of the year, we met with the psychologist. Colin was not a willing participant. He was suspicious and refused to answer some questions. Even with the emerging issues around attention, Colin's unwillingness to be tested was out of character. I realize that now. When the day was over, we were promised a written report with the results. We expected it to take some time, but after several months we were more than frustrated and called to ask when we might expect the report. The psychologist had forgotten to do it. About a month later, we were called by his office. The written report was available. Could we come in for a debriefing?

During the debriefing, the psychologist indicated that if we went to church, our home life would be "more stable" and that would be better for Colin. The implication was that Colin had learning challenges because we had opted away from organized religion. I was furious! Our home life was very stable. I appreciate people with devout religious beliefs, but I thought then as I do now that there is no place for religion in a psycho-educational assessment.

The psychologist also told us that because Colin had

refused to complete some questions, several sections were invalid and could not be used. The only definitive statement he made was that Colin was not affected by Attention Deficit Hyperactivity Disorder (ADHD). Ironically, we would realize a few years later that he was significantly affected by attention issues. We privately paid over a thousand dollars for a report we could not use, were insulted by the assertion that we did not have a stable home life but comforted by the erroneous finding that our son did not have ADHD.

In retrospect, we should have called the College of Psychologists in our province to complain about what had transpired. But, we did not have the energy for a fight. The bill had long since been paid, and we had more important things to do, like be good parents to our sons. But we did share our experience with our family doctor, believing he might want to re-think whether he would refer any other parents to this particular psychologist. The tragedy was that Colin's learning disability would go unrealized for another two years. We did the right thing in pursuing testing. If the testing had been done well, we would have learned much earlier about Colin's learning disabilities. But, that did not work out. Sadly, in the end it was Colin who suffered.

Despite our experience, I would strongly encourage any parent concerned with their child's progress to consider a psycho-educational assessment. A good assessment can provide critical information. For both young and older students, assessments offer vital insight into how a person learns. They can also provide the information necessary to diagnose many learning disabilities. However, this advice comes with a buyer beware caution. Not all psychologists are equal or skilled in this area. Consider seeking out referrals from local chapters of Learning Disabilities Associations. They often maintain a list of psychologists who provide quality assessments. If you have a bad experience, give that feedback to the association who provided you with the referral.

During grade one, we also encountered difficulties with a teaching assistant involved with Colin's education. In the program in which Colin was enrolled, each family was automatically a member of a non-profit society that raised money to pay for program enrichments, including teaching assistants. In Colin's class, there was both a teacher and a teacher's assistant, the latter employed by the parents. The relationship between Colin and the assistant began well, but steadily deteriorated as the year progressed. It caused all of us a great deal of angst.

The teacher's assistant was hired because she had expertise in the arts. She was personable but completely out of her depth when it came to addressing Colin's educational needs. Her passion and avocation was music. As Colin fell further and further behind his peers, he spent more and more time with her for one on one tutoring. With poor phonemic awareness and undiagnosed ADHD, the sessions were doomed to failure. The teaching assistant had little idea of what to do to help Colin. I suspect she had no training in special needs education and certainly no technical understanding of the issues around learning disabilities.

Colin was disheartened and increasingly resentful of the pull outs with the teaching assistant. He tried hard to complete the work sheets and was repeatedly admonished to "try harder." He has since told us he feels that the connection between his brain and the hand that holds his pencil does not work; he has severe dysgraphia and that issue was evident at an early age. We were angered to discover that the teacher's assistant had begun drawing "unhappy or sad faces" on the pages of printing Colin had worked so hard to complete. The teacher was mortified when she discovered this mode of feedback. The practice was immediately stopped.

Paul and I were becoming far more confident about advocating for Colin. The actions of the teaching assistant, if left unchecked, would have accelerated the decline that was already beginning to occur in Colin's self esteem and confidence as a learner. When criticisms come from "important adults," they carry more weight. Children, particularly in the early elementary grades, do not come to school each morning trying to think of ways they can get into trouble or irritate the adults in their lives. Quite the contrary. Most children want to learn and do well. I know Colin did.

All we need to do is to help our son "catch up" and other misperceptions

We were advised to practice writing with Colin by having him use his fingers to outline letters in either sand or rice. The message was that we should explore other media to help him learn to print. There was no systematic support to help him learn phonemes or letter sounds.

The second progress report in grade one clearly identified Colin's struggles as did the Highest Level of Achievement Tests (HLATs), administered that spring by the school district. They revealed Colin was performing far below expectations. As a result, he was placed in a school program to support students who were not doing well in language arts. A few mornings each week, he spent time with a delightful senior who would read one on one with students who had been identified to be "at risk." Colin enjoyed the time with Miss Betty, but the experience was no different from the reading we did with him every morning at school or every evening before bed. Colin had been exposed to books from a very early age. His reading problems were not a result of lack of books in his environment.

Every evening we would work with Colin to review his lessons and see if we could provide him with the support to "catch up." I visited the Teacher's Book Depository with sufficient frequency to know its layout. We had enough educational material to start our own elementary school. But I was Colin's mother and not his grade one teacher. I did not have an elementary education degree.

Throughout this entire period we were married to the idea that all we needed was to help Colin "catch-up." Once we did that, we thought everything would be fine. Armed with the information from the Hall and Moats book, we went looking for a tutoring or a summer program that would provide Colin with a sound foundation in phonemics. We found such an agency and enrolled him with the hopes that he would finally be able to "catch-up."

Five less teeth and breaking code
An eventful summer

Our mantra was that if we helped Colin catch up, everything would be fine. We pushed aside niggling doubts that there was something significant impacting his ability to learn.

The private agency we selected, based on the criteria from the Hall and Moats book, provided intense one on one support to students struggling to read and write. We scheduled a number of appointments in August. But we reserved a portion of July for a long overdue summer holiday to visit family in Ontario!

Paul has legions of extended family in the Hamilton-Toronto-Orillia area. My sister Charon lived just outside Brantford. We spent time in the lake country around Orillia enjoying its wonderful summer amenities. We saw very old and very young relatives, ate far too much and forgot about worries for a while. We took Colin and Kyle to Gravenhurst — a village that "houses" Santa's summer home. Colin was still pretending to believe in old St. Nick and Kyle was in awe of seeing the summer home where Mr. and Mrs. Claus lived.

I have bittersweet memories from this trip. We had a

chance to spend some very pleasant days with my sister Charon. It was the last time I would see her healthy; she died two years after our visit. Any time I subsequently spent with her was affected by her ever present companion, cancer. Charon and her husband took the boys for a memorable fishing expedition. Colin enthusiastically tried to cast his fishing line with too much force and too little style. The line came back in an arch and the hook got caught in his crotch! Fortunately, he was wearing heavy shorts and no harm was done! But, the near accident was a source of great amusement for younger brother Kyle.

As the vacation progressed, Colin struggled. He had a bit of a cold and mild fever. He complained his teeth were hurting. The former we attributed to a mild virus and the latter to the age appropriate process of losing baby teeth. He slept during the entire bus tour of the Safari Park outside Brantford, and woke up long enough to see Niagara Falls, seemingly affected by the medicine we gave him for his cold. He rallied when we arrived home, though he continued to make the occasional comment about his teeth. His complaints did not signify the very serious health issue which he narrowly avoided.

Within days of arriving home, Colin began tutoring sessions at the private agency. They based their instruction on the Lindamood-Bell Phonological Sequencing (LiPS) system. LiPS had its roots in the Orton-Gillingham Method — OGM for short — a multimodal program emphasizing phonemic awareness. LiPS focuses on enhancing phonological awareness, including training students to be aware of speech sounds in words and non-words, and uses oral-motor articulatory feed-back. Both OGM and LiPS focus on providing students with knowledge of the code that makes up language.

Colin was motivated to learn to read. He was fully aware he was behind his classmates in reading and writing. He demonstrated enthusiasm for his lessons and seemed to be making real progress. He emerged one Friday morning after his regular session to tell me, almost in a panicked manner that his teeth hurt so much that we would need to do some-thing about it right away. We had experienced many visits to the hospital for ill health associated with asthma and ear infections. Colin was not prone to exaggerate his symptoms. We learned that if he complained, he usually was ill. Our dentist was out of town so I phoned the emergency dental clinic at the hospital. Though an emergency clinic, patients needed to make appointments to be seen, a bit of a contra-diction to be certain, but I begged them to squeeze him in.

X-rays revealed he had an abscess around his teeth in his upper jaw that was beginning to spread. There was no outwards evidence of the infection. He had not spiked a fever and the dentist indicated how fortunate it was that we had come in for treatment when we did, or the situation might have been much more serious. A sedative was administered and he had five baby teeth extracted. We went home loaded with strong antibiotics and pain killers. We thought back to his mild complaints about his teeth during our trip, and suffered pangs of retroactive guilt. Could we have done something sooner?

Colin continued with his summer program after his dental surgery. He must have been challenged to speak with any level of articulatory precision because he had five fewer teeth. However, the program was a huge success and led to an event we will never forget.

One evening, about two weeks after he had started the sessions, and well past his bed time, Colin came excitedly into our bedroom with a book in hand. It was a large font early reader book — something he had been unable to conquer during grade one. He exclaimed, "I can read!" Without waiting for a response from us, he began to read aloud, from cover to cover, the little book tightly gripped in his hands. He had broken the code! That night was emotional for us. We saw in the face of our son, pride in his accomplishment and unfettered enjoyment in being able to read.

Grade two
Déjà vu all over again!

Colin was excited about his newfound reading ability and was looking forward to grade two! His teacher was the same as grade one and she let Colin know how proud she was of him for his work over the summer.

Preparations for back to school in our household were in high gear that year as Kyle was also starting school! He was set to begin full day kindergarten in the same school as Colin. Both boys were also in the out of school care program.

I was enthused about the new school year. On a personal note, my business was busy and flourishing. My sister in Ontario was judged to be cancer free. Kyle was adapting well to kindergarten, though he occasionally indicated that perhaps he would not go to school, thinking somehow that it was an optional activity.

The bubble burst pretty quickly. Violating every principle of the space — time continuum, Colin ended up being a month behind after only two weeks of school. We had been so sure that all he needed to do was catch up. But, once again, Colin was simply not progressing at the same pace as his peers.

He was being severely hampered by his dysgraphia as the grade two curriculum placed a much heavier emphasis on writing. His pleasure at returning to school quickly evaporated. We were fortunate that throughout grade one, his self esteem, though fragile, had remained relatively intact. But early in grade two, it took a nose dive. He began to ask difficult questions: "I am trying really hard. Why are the other kids doing so much better than me?" We wondered the same thing.

We consistently reinforced to Colin our belief in him. We told him he was very smart. It was excruciating to watch as a parent; it must have been extremely difficult for him to live through this experience. Very early in grade two, Paul and I felt it was important to arrange for Colin to get additional support outside school. We considered having him return to the agency where he had learned to read in the summer. But that option was very expensive. It would also require that he miss school for parts of the day to accommodate the sessions. We wanted to keep school as normal as possible for him and so we abandoned that option. We were referred to a teacher who was a reading specialist and had training in the Orton-Gillingham method. She had worked as a teaching assistant in the alternative program in which Colin was enrolled and came with stellar recommendations. We engaged her to tutor Colin. The support, 90 minutes every Saturday morning, was successful in slowing the pace with which he was falling behind. But, he continued to fall behind in anything that required writing. Reading, while not one of his strengths, remained something he enjoyed.

As a side note, the financial burden of purchasing private support was accumulating. It began when we engaged private speech therapists. At that time, the cost of therapy was about $60-$80 per hour. His therapy at ISTAR exceeded $3000. The cost of the summer agency where Colin learned to read was about the same as ISTAR. Individual tutoring was about $60-80 per hour. In a two and a half year period, we spent about $10,000 in treatment and educational resources to help Colin.

Grade two was such a complicated year. There was a new teaching assistant. He was a kind man, but he too, was completely out of his depth in addressing Colin's needs. As a student indentified at risk for reading problems, Colin continued to read with Miss Betty, an activity he enjoyed. But, there was no specific focus on the technical elements that were creating Colin's problems with reading and writing. Colin's teacher was stretched. Some of the new grade one students had behavior issues, consuming a great deal of her time. Colin was well behaved; he blended into the pack. The teacher was aware he was getting outside support from a person she respected. I suspect she felt his needs were being addressed. She concentrated on the other students with exceptional learning needs.

I continued to be an active volunteer in the class. It was clear, even to my untrained eye that a number of children were struggling with reading and writing. There was a small budget surplus in the parent community coffers and I put forward the suggestion, with the backing of the teacher and parent community president, that the surplus be used to engage the tutor to come into the class and work intensely with children who were struggling. I regarded the proposal as an enrichment, consistent with the program's mission, and one infinitely more valuable than an additional field trip.

One parent was a whole language proponent. She was against the option because the tutor would be using the Orton-Gillingham method. Though I disagreed with her about OGM, I respected her opinion. However, I was not prepared for the response of other parents who did not want to spend money for the tutor, because, in the words of one, "Their child was not 'defective' like ours." I was dumfounded. I would subsequently encounter parents who felt that students with exceptional learning needs siphoned resources away from 'normal' students, whatever normal might be. But this was the first time I encountered this view.

If it's not one thing, it's another

In the midst of this crazy year, health issues emerged for Colin. Tutoring presented us with a health challenge. The tutor had cats. She only tutored out of her house. Colin was allergic to cats.

Colin began to have more and more difficulties breathing during and after these sessions. After the debacle where the parent community resoundingly indicated they did not want the tutor to support at risk students in Colin's class, she was reluctant to go to the school. She would not tutor in a child's home. We were forced to discontinue the sessions before Christmas. We figured breathing trumped reading.

Shortly after Christmas, Colin began complaining about non-specific stomach pains. He was not enjoying school. His complaints were not repeated or adamant and we attributed them to stress. However, a week later, the school called us saying he was ill. He had developed a high fever. We sought immediate medical attention and learned he had bilateral pneumonia. He had likely been walking around with the condition for some time. We suffered retroactive guilt; we were dumbfounded that once again, Colin had been struck by a significant health issue under our watchful eyes.

Over the next few years, he would be affected by multiple bouts of pneumonia. Our family doctor coached me on how to identify signs of reoccurrence. On more than one occasion at the Emergency Department, I would caution pediatric residents about how Colin could look healthy and be ill. They tended to come around after they read his chest x-rays. Colin suffered three bouts of pneumonia between Christmas and the end of school. Our family doctor referred him to a host of specialists, including an allergist, otolaryngologist — a physician specializing in ear-nose-and throat surgery, and a pediatric pulmonologist.

The ENT specialist had the people skills of a barracuda. He was somewhat perplexed that our eight year old son, with no preparation, was resistant about having an endoscopic camera snaked up his nose to examine his nasal passages and sinuses. I was able to convince Colin to "let the tube with the camera" go up his nose. He was frightened and clamped tightly onto my hand throughout the procedure. But, he made it through. The scope revealed that he had extensive polyps which would likely require surgery. We were also told, to our horror, that nasal polyps were uncommon *except* among children with cystic fibrosis. So, off we went for testing for CF. Our relief was palpable when we learned the tests were negative. Also ordered, a CT scan of the sinuses to determine how far up the polyps went beyond the reach of the endoscopic camera. The results of the CT scan suggested the possible need for surgery in the future — once he, and his nose, grew some more.

We also saw the allergist. He prescribed heavy duty steroids to reduce the nasal polyps. Steroids are not benign, and we were very concerned about their impact on his long term development. We held off getting the prescription filled.

The next doctor we saw was the pediatric pulmonologist. He was pragmatic, efficient, child friendly and highly approachable. In somewhat colorful language, he stated that in no way would he support a child of eight taking an extended dose of steroids for nasal polyps. He mumbled something about the prescribed course of action being equivalent to malpractice. This wonderful pulmonologist has seen our son through multiple cases of pneumonia and breathing issues, and to this day is a critical member of Colin's health care team.

All these events made grade two seem to go on forever. In the late spring, Paul and I made the decision to pull Colin from the program of choice and enroll him in a regular grade three class at Strathearn School. We were also able to find another tutor who had training in phonics. She tutored Colin, seeing him at the school before the end of the term and from our home in the summer months following grade two.

Colin was tired by the end of grade two. So were we. We felt isolated in our efforts to get him the help he needed. We knew something was wrong. We knew it was imperative that he be supported to become literate. We felt the burden of responsibility rested with us to educate Colin and make up for the deficits in his education. We felt compelled to become lay experts. The education system was clearly designed for children different from him. He was a square peg in a round hole — or so we thought. We were totally unaware that Colin had exceptional learning needs. We thought that only children with physical or mental health issues qualified for special education. We were two years away from knowing about the provincial Standards for Special Education that enshrine the right of accessibility to education for all children. The beginning of that summer marked a low point for our entire family.

Dog days of summer

Our family seemed to settle into another summer defined by Colin's educational needs.

He attended school from September to June. In July and August we focused our efforts on helping him catch up so that he would not be as far behind when school started again in the fall. Into July and the hot days of summer, Colin continued with tutoring two times a week. He was a trooper. He sincerely wanted to do better, and was highly motivated. His brother, a new graduate of kindergarten, did "school work" during Colin's tutoring sessions. During the first two weeks of July, Kyle managed to successfully make his way through a grade one language arts work book! Unlike Colin, reading and writing was very easy for Kyle. If the birth order of our two sons had been reversed, we would have appreciated at a much earlier age the extent of Colin's struggles.

We tried to intersperse tutoring with summer fun. But after a few weeks, Colin began resisting the tutoring. One day, after the tutor left, he said to me, "I just want to fly into the sun." He was depressed and frustrated. And, we were making it worse in our efforts to help him. The tutor was scheduled to go on a holiday and we ended the sessions earlier than planned. We questioned if we were doing the right thing.

I began a more concerted effort to gain expertise. I read extensively. I browsed the parenting and education section at bookstores. During this process, I discovered a book that described "dyslexia" as a gift. I was attracted to its title. It contained a list of characteristics typical of individuals with dyslexia or other learning disabilities. The list comprehensively described Colin. I read it aloud to Paul, commenting on how it aptly matched our son. Paul immediately dismissed my conclusions, saying, "Half of those things apply to me!" My response back to him was, "None of those things apply to me." It was a defining moment that Paul and I will always remember.

We now know learning disabilities run in families; it can have a heritable component. We discovered Paul, with multiple university degrees and a stratospheric IQ is impacted by learning disabilities, though not as severely as Colin. In addition to insight, the book gave us optimism. Its message was clear and unequivocal; interventions existed to help people like Colin.

I hit the internet and discovered a trainer in Calgary for the program described in the book. That internet search also led me to the site for a private school in Calgary that specialized in students with learning disabilities. I decided to check it out. I was told Colin would need a psycho-educational assessment indicating he had learning disabilities to gain admission to the school. But, neither the psycho-educational assessment nor the educators in Colin's life said that he had learning disabilities.

Because of this, we erroneously thought his learning needs were not serious enough to be granted access to such a school or to special education supports.

We planned a family road trip to Calgary to visit the zoo, see the sites, and meet with the trainer. The intervention consisted of using clay to mold out letters. I recognized this process as being neurological imprinting, and could appreciate, in abstract, the way it worked. We were advised there was a certified trainer in Edmonton and when we returned home, we connected with her.

Colin had one week of intense intervention doing the clay modeling therapy. It was fun for him — a definite break from the earlier work. Whether it benefited him in any way, we are not sure. But the instructor was caring, genuine in her belief in the system, and adding to our growing knowledge about dyslexia. In a spirit of continuing denial or ignorance, we somehow failed to appreciate that dyslexia was a learning disability. We also failed to appreciate that Colin had other neuro-processing characteristics consistent with learning disabilities.

That summer, our family also played host to all living members of my family of origin. Charon had recovered suffi-ciently from her chemotherapy to travel to visit us. Nancy flew in from British Columbia, and the three of us had a wonderful and bittersweet time together. Nancy and I had a premonition that Charon would succumb to cancer. We wanted the time together to reconnect and celebrate life. Midway through the visit we were joined by my father and his wife. My father had remarried a few years earlier. It was the last time we would all be together.

Grade three
Angels as teachers and sisters as angels

Ultimately, September rolled around and it was back to school. Kyle marched into grade one armed with a binder of work he had completed over the summer. Colin was in a grade two-three split class, something that pleased us immensely.

Colin was still very much behind his peers, and we thought that split would be easier for him. Good fortune was smiling on our family that day in the person of his teacher, Kristen Bowal, an angel on earth masquerading as a teacher. Paul and I are certain her actions that year saved Colin's life.

Kristen is a very organized teacher. That year, all the students in her class participated in a home reading program. Colin loved this aspect of grade three. He actually got credit for reading at home — something he did everyday anyway. Weekly homework packages and spelling lists were handed out on Monday. Homework was due on Friday. This gave us a chance to work with Colin and plan for the week. Spelling quizzes were also on Friday. We devised a process for practicing spelling that involved both Colin and Kyle. We pretended they were competing on a TV game show.

Colin was devastated with his initial report card. It was bad but it was honest. He received low marks in most subjects except Art. Unknown to us, he approached Kristen to tell her that he believed he could do better. He asked for her help to improve. She made arrangements to meet Colin every day after school for a week. Fuelled by snacks she brought for the occasion, Colin and Kristen identified about 15 strategies that would support Colin's goal for improvement. These strategies were then listed in a column on a table that also had columns for each day of the week. The table, which was refreshed weekly, was taped to Colin's desk. Each day, after school ended, Colin and Kristen would meet and place a check mark beside strategies he had successfully used that day. The goals were practical and age appropriate. They included things like not losing his pencil, important for a child with attentional issues, through to participating in class discussions.

Colin would come home on a really good day, proudly announcing that he had earned 12 or 13 check marks! When he had bad days, Kristen would remind him he was capable of achieving his goals, and she had faith that tomorrow would be a better day. The strategies, or mini goals, were modified after the second report card, using a similar process.

He improved immensely. The most dramatic change was in math. He went from a D during the first term, to a B in the second, and then to an A for the final term. To this day, he self identifies as being good in mathematics.

Midway through the second term, Kristen caught me in

the hallway and asked if I could speak to her. It was the end of the day, and I was in the school to pick up the boys from after school care. She acknowledged Colin was making progress but felt he was struggling and could do better. She highlighted his strengths — something I sincerely appreciated. She indicated it was her job to do the best she could to teach Colin. She said that there were things going on with him from an educational standpoint that were beyond her understanding. She wanted to ask our permission to consult with experts from the school district to test Colin so that she, and in fact all of us, could gain a better understanding about his learning needs. Without any reservations at all, we supported her proposal for testing.

I serve, on occasion, as a guest lecturer for fourth-year students in the Faculty of Education at the University of Alberta. I speak about approaching parents of children with exceptional needs. I indicate that the manner Kristen broached this subject with me is exemplary and could be used as a model for speaking with parents.

Kristen Bowal was a ray of hope in the midst of an otherwise difficult year. In November, my sister Charon had routine scans resulting in a declaration that she was cancer free. By December, there were obvious signs that the cancer had returned. In mid January, she complained about constant abdominal pain and saw her doctor. Before the scheduled dates for tests to investigate her pain, she was rushed to hospital. The cancer was back with a vengeance and had metastasized to her liver. She had 13 tumors ranging in size from grapes to golf balls.

I was the first of our family to fly to Ontario to visit her.
I took her to her first and only chemotherapy session; she was
too sick to have any more treatments. Charon and I spoke
frankly about her likely impending death. She told me that she
was not afraid to die, but that she did not want to die at such a
young age. I was the luckiest of our family. I was able to spend
time with her before she became confused, a side effect of the
toxins circulating in her system that her liver could no longer
remove.

Shortly after I left, Nancy, my other sister, flew out to see
Charon. The deterioration in her condition was pronounced.
The task fell to me, with support from Nancy, to tell my father
that Charon was dying and that he should be prepared to say
good bye. My father and his wife remained with her in the final
two weeks of her life. She died six weeks after she was initially
rushed to hospital.

Charon's battle and death from cancer was a central aspect
of our life during that difficult time. The need for a parent to
advocate for a child occurs within the backdrop of life. In some
rare cases, a family's life is uncomplicated and meeting the
needs of a child may be a parent's sole concern. But, I suspect
that in the majority of cases, parents must juggle many things
at the same time. To educators, psychologists, physicians,
and the myriad of others who deal with parents struggling
to support their children, it is important to be sensitive to the
context of a parent's life. I know I was not at my best at that
time. I was emotionally fragile. My sister has been dead for

six years, and at times, I am still moved to tears. I am grateful that in the midst of this very difficult year for us, our son was blessed with a teacher like Kristen.

Before her death, Charon and I spoke frequently on the phone. She knew Colin had been referred for testing. She began to send me links to inspirational articles about children who had overcome learning challenge to become successful. Her death prevented her from knowing the outcome of the testing.

Is he in? Yes, no, possibly so!

The testing took place over several weeks. Colin actually enjoyed the process. He indicated it was nice to speak to adults who seemed to understand how he thought. He said they gave him advice about how to do his school work.

We were not aware, until a bit later in the process, that the testing outcomes would also be used to determine whether he was eligible to receive special education supports within our school district. In most school districts, there are generally three options for educational venues for students with exceptional learning needs. A student can remain in a regular classroom in a community school where the classroom teacher addresses the student's unique learning needs. This educational option is generally referred to as *inclusion*. The second option is for a student to attend a community school but receive core subjects (language arts, math, science and social studies) with a cohort of other students also assessed as having an exceptional learning need. Within this setting, other classes like art, physical education, etc. are integrated with the rest of the student body. This type of venue is referred to as a *congregated* setting. The final option is an educational venue where all children have exceptional learning needs such as learning disabilities. This option is referred to as a *segregated* environment — a term I hate. I prefer the term, *"specialized site."* All three were available to us within our school district as possible educational venues for Colin.

When Colin was being tested, our school district had very strict criteria to determine eligibility for special education programming for learning disabilities. Different school districts will have different criteria. To qualify for support, Colin needed to be at the 10th percentile or lower in two or more subjects. He needed to have an IQ of 100 or more, considered to be average. To continue to get special education support, he had to stay below the 20th percentile in two or more subjects.

These standards reflect the "wait to fail" mentality that permeates many of our school systems. "Waiting to fail" is comparable to using a band-aid on a very large flesh wound just as a patient is dying from blood loss. It is certainly not about maximizing the educational potential of each child.

I was flabbergasted about the rigid entry level criteria! Colin, or any child, needed to fail miserably to get help to succeed. It seemed draconian to me. Even with my lack of familiarity with learning disabilities, I could not help but think that eligibility should be based on need, and that the unique characteristics of a child should be considered. I was starting to gain some understanding of the policy quagmire of the current state of special education. The cynical side of me said it was about money. My views then were that these criteria were designed to ration programming rather than meeting needs.

When Colin's results came back, we discovered he was on the bubble. At the 10.5th percentile, he was deemed ineligible for special education programming or supports. Our reaction was shock. He was so close but so far away. We felt our efforts to help him had backfired; he most certainly would have scored below the 10th percentile without the tutoring and active support we provided. All that mattered was the number. I still suffer retroactive anger about his near miss. There were several difficult days for us, with my mood made even darker by Charon's recent death.

Then a miracle happened. I have a few ideas about what might have generated the miracle, and no, it did not involve heavenly intervention but actions by humans. Somehow his test results were recalculated and he was found to be at the 10th percentile. Our relief was palpable.

Many weeks transpired from the time the testing occurred to when the recalculated results were made known to us. Our first choice for an educational venue, the Academy at King Edward (AKE), a specialized site within the public system, was full. Colin was put on the waiting list. We were very clear that we wanted him to go to the Academy. We did not believe inclusion was the best option for him; he had experienced the best possible inclusive environment in grade three with his teacher Kristen Bowal. If he could not flourish in her classroom, we believed it unlikely he would do well in a regular classroom. There was a congregated program close to our home. However, it was located in the school we had dismissed when interviewing principals before Colin began kindergarten. It was the school where we had witnessed the boy receiving medication without being greeted or spoken to by the adults in the room. It was also where the principal had admonished me about asking questions about Colin's needs. That same principal was still at the school located mere blocks from our home.

We spoke to parents whose children had or currently were attending the Academy. One parent had been one of my clients. My question to him: "Do we embrace this educational opportunity or do we run away from it as fast as we can?" The answer, "You embrace the opportunity and feel fortunate in doing so." My client and his wife joined us for beverages one evening and explained why we should consider AKE. The most important reason they cited — the staff at the school. They described them as "special." That proved to be exactly the case.

Even though Colin was on the wait list, we were invited for a tour of the school, the equivalent of an open house. This tour entailed two or three prospective students meeting with a senior staff member to see the school and get excited about coming. We wondered if we should accept the invitation...we did not want to raise expectations unless there was a good chance Colin would be attending the school. But, we ultimately decided the school administration would not have invited us unless it was likely that there was a space for him.

In the midst of all of this, we forgot something important —
Colin's view about a change in schools! He was not keen, to say
the least, about going to AKE. He loved Strathearn School. He
was very comfortable in out of school care. This was a wrinkle
we should have anticipated but did not. I tried enticement and
showed him the school's website. He was most impressed with
the student showcase and wondered if his work would ever
be good enough to be showcased. We had him hooked. Some
of his art ultimately did make it up on the site. When the day
arrived for the orientation, Colin was surprised to see one of
his classmates in the hallway. Unknown to him, this student
had also been undergoing testing and was also going to this
new school.

Time marched on. One day, about three weeks after the
tour, the phone rang. It was the principal of our existing school
telling us Colin was off the wait list! We attended the parent
orientation a few weeks later, and were warmly welcomed by
the Principal and Assistant Principal. It was the end of both a
remarkably good and horrible year for our family. It was also
the start of a new chapter for Colin.

Thank you J.K. Rowling!

In the summer months after grade three and before Colin started at the Academy, Paul, in a frustrated moment, decided to cut our cable tv service.

A representative of the cable company was going up and down our street to let us all know that somehow the company had not charged us for a particular tier of channels. Essentially we were getting channels for free that none of us watched anyway and now our bills would be adjusted upwards. It was a wonderful spring Saturday, and Paul was somewhat frustrated with the boys' lack of enthusiasm for being outside enjoying the Alberta sunshine. He inquired if there would be any diffi-culties in quickly reinstating cable if we cut it off that morning. Learning it could be reinstalled in a heartbeat and after a quick check with me, cable service was discontinued!

We did not announce this decision to Colin or Kyle, but it did not take long before they emerged from the basement to say, "The TV downstairs is not working! None of them are working!" Our reply, "We know. We cut the cable." This was one of those moments when it was a good thing that we had two children because that way they could complain to each other about their terrible parents!

It started out a bit hard, but after a few days, the withdrawal symptoms abated a bit and the kids got into a wonderful routine. The park at the end of the street was much more enticing. Swimming took on a new cachet. Somehow, their rooms were much cleaner. And, both kids loved nothing better than to curl up with books.

We started reading aloud the Harry Potter series by J.K. Rowling. Taking on the Harry Potter series was a significant commitment. In addition to reading Harry Potter, we also read aloud *Eragon* by Christopher Paolini. Colin and Kyle were somewhat in awe that Paolini had written *Eragon* when he was fifteen years old.

Though Colin enjoyed reading, he was overwhelmed by "real books." He confined his reading to chapter books with large font and pictures. He would become somewhat hysterical if we suggested he read anything longer than a chapter book. If he had his way, he would try to get us to read the chapter books to him rather than read them himself. For him, a full page of text was daunting.

We began, of course, with *Harry Potter and the Philosopher's Stone*. Paul and I shared reading responsibility, though Paul preferred that I read and he listen. The books are quite wonderful to read out loud, and when Paul or I had raw throats and wanted to stop, we would be encouraged by the boys saying "Just one more chapter," or "Just a few more pages!"

A few days into book one of Harry Potter, Colin asked if he could read ahead by himself. He said, "I just can't get enough of this book." We encouraged him to do so, and with the book, he went off to his room to read. He tried very hard. But, the print on the book was small, about ten point font. Colin indicated he had trouble following where he was on the page. He expressed frustration that the print seemed to fall off the side of the page.

Visual perception issues are not uncommon among children/readers with learning disabilities. For some readers, the letters swim or bounce in front of their eyes. For others, like Colin, the words seem to fall off the side of the page. Other visual challenges are when the spaces between words create white rivers down the centre of a page, and this visual perception interferes with the reading experience. As you might expect, all make it difficult to read.

Colin did not have a problem with larger text and I got the brain wave that large print books, designed for people with low or poor vision, might do the trick. We kept up the pace with reading the series aloud. But I also set out on a mission to find the Harry Potter series in large print. It was a challenge. Large print books in our city's public library were confined to adult books and romance novels; there were few large print youth oriented books. It appeared to me, confirmed by a kind librarian I had enlisted for help, that as soon as children graduate from chapter books, font size shrinks to ten or eleven point font. Not to be deterred, I went to my book store and was able to find a large print version of *The Philosopher's Stone* for a price roughly equivalent to three of the original books. The results were immediate. Colin was much more comfortable reading the large print books. So I set out to purchase the rest of the Harry Potter series in large print.

I managed to find large print versions of three of the five published books. Time pressures were upon us. We were missing the large print version of *The Prisoner of Azkaban* and were almost half way through the second book in the series, *The Chamber of Secrets. Azkaban* was next! I ordered it online, with it arriving in a nick of time. When we were not reading as a family, Colin would take the books and would read ahead, or reread the sections we had shared as a family. On a personal note, something most adults with progressive lenses will appreciate, it was much more pleasurable reading aloud from a large print book.

We owe a thank you to J.K. Rowling for the role she played in facilitating Colin's transition to "regular books." She has been a lightning rod for reading amongst our youth. I have been told by many parents that their children, particularly their sons, really got hooked on books by reading Harry Potter. Colin made the huge jump that summer because he was so engaged in the series.

There is a somewhat funny side bar to the summer of Harry Potter. Colin is fair minded and empathetic. With a spoiler alert to those of you who may not have read *The Goblet of Fire*, Colin was angered when Cedric Diggory died on the order of the evil Lord Voldemort. His reaction was immediate and definitive: "She's killed Cedric Diggory and I am done with J.K. Rowling! She should not have killed him off!" He left the large print version of the *Order of the Phoenix* unread. However, he did "listen in" from the other room when we read the book aloud to Kyle. He also came to the midnight parties for the release of the final two books in the series. Somehow, he has a firm understanding of the Harry Potter plot and all its intrigues!

Large print books, though difficult to find, may be considered for a select group of students to help them transition to regular books. It worked for Colin. In less than a year, he was comfortable with regular books that were not large print.

And so our summer ended. We did reinstate cable. We waited for the kids to discover that it was back on. We knew that every now and then, they checked to see if it had mysteriously returned.

Early days at the Academy

We were beginning to get used to the reality that Colin had learning disabilities. It was gradual; I cannot define one particular moment when we moved into the stage of acceptance. But, it did happen.

We took the summer off, or more specifically, Colin was not subjected to the summer ritual of tutoring to help him catch up before the start of the new school year. It was blissful for us — the adults in his life. Ironically, in a pattern that would be repeated summer after summer, Colin demonstrated difficulties adapting to a more relaxed schedule. He was more comfortable in a very structured environment, something that persists to this day.

We engaged in all the regular back to school preparation — new clothes, new supplies, new hope. The focus on organization was evident from a look at the supply list for grade four students. It came with very specific instructions about the shape of pens, size of binders, color coded duo tangs, and on and on. We would come to learn that the supplies were used to help organize the study and work habits of students, and in so doing enhance their executive function.

For the first time ever, Colin would be taking a school bus. As a child enrolled in a special education program, he was eligible for curbside yellow bus transit and we decided we would use this service. The plan was for the bus to pick him up at our house in the morning; at the end of the day, he would take another bus to Strathearn School where he would attend out of school care with Kyle. We believed he would be returning to Strathearn and wanted him to have a chance to maintain relationships with other children. The convenience factor was that we would be able to pick up both Colin and Kyle at the same place at the end of our work day.

We engaged in a divide and conquer strategy that first day of school. I stuck with Colin and Paul accompanied Kyle to his first day of grade two! Fortunately, we already knew that Kyle would have Kristen Bowal as a teacher. We thought we would be in for a very uneventful year at Strathearn. That assumption was wrong; that year saw us in the middle of a huge battle to keep the school from closing.

Like legions of other parents, I was off in the car as soon as the bus left our doorstep to see it arrive at AKE with Colin. I carried with me two large bags of school supplies. When I arrived at the school, I was one of a crowd of parents doing the same thing. Colin and I entered the school to find his appointed classroom. We were both greeted by his new teacher and a teaching assistant. The process was similar to schools across the continent. It was a dance of orchestrated confusion and the normalcy was comforting. The teacher was as adept at dealing with nervous parents as she was with apprehensive students.

I was nervous the entire day. I arrived at the out of school care program at Strathearn before Colin had even arrived on the bus. When I saw him, he indicated that the day had gone very well, commenting, "All the kids are just like me!" Instead of feeling like an outsider, he felt like he belonged. He made mention of one particular boy with whom he had spent some time that day.

The first few weeks were a blur. We were getting used to our responsibilities as parents of a child in this new program. But in the early weeks of the school year, tragedy struck. One Monday morning in late September, the students in Colin's class were advised that his new friend's father had been tragically killed the previous Friday. Grief counselors were on hand to support all the children. Colin had an extremely hard time with the news — much more so than the other students. I received a call from the school principal, Rob Cameron, to let me know about Colin's reaction.

I had met Rob on a few occasions in the months before Colin started at the Academy. I have the highest level of res- pect for him as an educator and person. Colin was so lucky to have him at the helm of the school, and we benefited in so many ways from his guidance and observations.

Rob outlined what happened in his call, and told me that he was with both Colin and the boy who had just lost his father. We agreed to monitor the situation. The two boys joined Rob for lunch in his office, an environment rich with items much loved by student visitors. The office was the antithesis of the stern and uninviting principal's office; it was an inviting and safe haven. As the day progressed, Rob and I decided it would be best if I came to take Colin home early.

When I got to the school, Rob asked me if I had some insight into Colin's reaction. As I began to tell him that I suspected it was due to the recent death of Charon, his Aunt, I began to cry. It was something over which I had no control — it just happened. Poor Rob! Not only was he dealing with an extremely difficult situation in a class at the school and the need to support a child who had lost his father. He now had a crying parent in his office. While I was able to collect myself relatively quickly, I have vivid memories of the feelings that hit me at that particular moment.

I believe, much more strongly now than I did at that time, that the quality of a school is a direct reflection of the people who make up its staff. Technical skills are essential — and the staff at AKE were specialists in teaching students with learning disabilities. But compassion is also an incredibly important element. Compassion was showed to me, to our son, and to the other children in Colin's class on that day.

Many students with exceptional learning needs have "baggage." Their self-esteem may be low and they may feel like they can do nothing. But having "baggage" is not the exclusive domain of children. Parents can be battered and bruised from their journey of support for their children. In the meantime, life and death happens. It was a part of our family's reality.

I feel like a new man today!
Taking medication for ADHD

We all settled into the new reality of our life. Kyle was thriving in grade two and Colin loved AKE. We took a few minutes to catch our breath.

It is funny that I have clear memories of events affecting Colin before he entered the Academy. However, I struggle to remember details from the early part of grade four — the first year Colin was at AKE. I think the blurring of my memory was because this period was a more relaxed time for Paul and me. For the first time in years, we were not fighting to get help for Colin. Our worry about his future, while present, was not a constant buzz in the background.

But normal, of course, is relative. It was autumn and a time of year when Colin's asthma frequently acted up. That year, his fall bout of asthma evolved into pneumonia. It required a few trips to the hospital emergency department. Even there, vigilance was necessary to ensure he received the care he needed.

Colin is large and looks healthy. In teaching hospitals, it is often a medical resident (a doctor in training) who is the first to evaluate a patient. The resident then reports or confers with the regular physician (the staff physician) who sees the patient next. Most often, the resident is the person responsible for ordering tests to help diagnosis a patient's condition.

That day, when the resident came to evaluate Colin, she initially indicated that he looked well. She listened to his lungs and could not hear anything unusual. Having gone through this drill before, I reminded her that his oxygen saturation level was low, something we knew from the tests conducted when we arrived at Emergency. I commented that he was the type of child who could fool doctors and appear healthy when he was not. She reluctantly ordered x-rays. The results were definitive — he had pneumonia in the lower lobes of both lungs! Colin was placed on third generation antibiotics and administered multiple doses of inhaled Ventolin to get his oxygen levels high enough to enable him to go home.

Colin is the veteran of multiple trips to Emergency. Fortunately, his asthma is controlled much better now, and hospital visits are infrequent. I was normally the one to take Colin to Emergency while Paul stayed home with Kyle. Hospitals are places characterized by intense periods of excitement followed by long stretches of extreme boredom. Children who are ill are not inclined to be creative about staying occupied during periods while awaiting test results or being monitored. Colin was no different.

During our frequent visits to the emergency department, to help pass the time, Colin and I made up a story about "The Purple People Eater." This character was inspired by the 1958 song "The One Eyed, One Horned Purple People Eater," written and recorded by Sheb Wooley. We gave the Purple People Eater life! It was the hospital story and one Colin and I shared. We took the old Purple People Eater on trips, made him into a vegetarian, and had him visit the library, invite people over for vegetarian lasagna and so on.

With treatment, Colin became healthier and returned to school. The school also had a parents' education program. Held every second Saturday morning over a period of two months, the program was created to educate parents about learning disabilities. Parents were provided with practical strategies on how to help their child. I attended the parent program during the fall, and Paul took the program in the winter. It is interesting that aspects of the program resonated differently for both of us.

The idea of teaching parents how to address their child's unique needs is brilliant. I learned a great deal from the program. But oddly, I left each session somewhat agitated and depressed. I believe it was because I was still learning to accept Colin's challenges. These sessions clearly reinforced his special needs. I think I was harboring some unspoken and unrecognized feelings that he would be "cured" and that his learning disabilities and their implications would not color the rest of his life. Clearly, he has a lifelong condition. But, at that time, it was hard for me to truly internalize that reality.

It was during a parent session that I learned Rick Lavoie, an accomplished speaker, author and educator in the field of learning disabilities, would deliver the keynote address at a conference in Red Deer, approximately 90 minutes down the highway. Paul and I decided that I should attend his presentation. During the parent sessions, the instructor had played a short segment of Lavoie's video, "How Hard Can it be? The F.A.T. City Workshop." FAT stands for Frustration, Anxiety and Tension. I was hooked. We borrowed the video from our library and watched it in its entirety. Viewing it was an emotional and cathartic experience. Produced in 1989, it remains as relevant now as it was then. Of particular importance to us was the way it described some of the emotions and frustrations of children with learning disabilities. The video helped us modify our parenting strategies to provide Colin with better support.

On the appointed day of the Lavoie lecture, I set off down the highway and entered the conference ballroom as a lone parent. I was not a member of the "community" and felt more alone than ever sitting by myself. Eventually, I saw a parent from Colin's school and we sat together — partners in the learning process. Lavoie started his presentation. It felt like he was speaking directly to me.

During that session, Lavoie raised the issue of how attention issues often co-exist with learning disabilities. The reality that Colin might have Attention Deficit Hyperactivity Disorder (ADHD) continued to bubble up and cause Paul and me concerns. We were worried he was affected by ADHD but the psychologist's assessment conducted when he was in grade one indicated this condition was not present. We attributed his variable focus as being an aspect of his learning disabilities rather than an issue onto itself. The Lavoie lecture caused us to re-examine this assumption.

Colin was still being monitored by the pediatric pulmonologist because of his most recent bout of pneumonia. A thorough and engaging physician, during any routine visit he always asked both Colin and me how things were going at school. It was this physician who bluntly told me Colin's learning disabilities would be lifelong. It was now this same physician who suggested a creative strategy to test the hypothesis that he had attentional issues.

We were not keen on medicating Colin. It might even be more accurate to say we were anti-medication. We had heard horror stories about children being "anesthetized" with medication. We also knew that Ritalin, a medication frequently used to treat ADHD, needed to be administered every few hours. While we had confidence in the administration of Colin's school, we did not want to label him as having yet another "problem." Colin's doctor advised us about an extended or sustained release (SR) version of Ritalin. This medication would only need to be given once a day, and his recommendation was that we might want to trial it for a short period to see whether it made a difference. Armed with this information, we went back to our family doctor and obtained a prescription.

It was now December. We decided to start the SR Ritalin on a weekend so we could carefully monitor its impact. We did not tell Colin what the pill was designed to do — we simply described it as another vitamin he had to take in the morning.

On the day we gave him the first dose, all of us attended a Christmas event in our community known as the Festival of Trees. Designer Christmas trees are created and auctioned off to the highest bidder in support of the local teaching hospital. The Festival of Trees is a wonderful feast for the eyes and ears — the public looks at beautiful trees while listening to seasonal music that permeates a huge conference hall. It is a great way to get into the holiday spirit.

That afternoon, as we were riding the elevator at the Conference Centre to the Festival, Colin turned to us and said, "I don't know what has happened but I feel like a new man today! I feel great!" Paul and I looked at each other, simultaneously feeling elated that the medication might work for Colin and horribly guilty that we had not considered treatment earlier. It turned out that it worked amazingly well — for a while. Initially, we did not tell his teacher or the school administration that Colin was taking medication for ADHD. Two weeks later, his teacher advised us that he seemed to be "settling down" and doing his work.

Ultimately, we had to take him off that particular type of sustained release Ritalin because it interfered dramatically with his sleep. The longer he took the medication, the longer he stayed awake at night. After about three months, we switched over to a non-stimulant and very expensive medication that did not work for him at all. Soon afterwards, with the support of the school, he began to take the immediate release Ritalin and continued on that therapy for some time. Now older and larger, he has returned to a new brand of SR Ritalin.

So, in addition to learning disabilities, we had confirmation that Colin also had ADHD. The estimates of individuals with learning disabilities who also have ADHD range from 30% to 50%. There is also evidence that people with ADHD who do not take medication are more likely to suffer from addiction to alcohol and other prescription and non-prescription drugs compared to people with ADHD who are medicated. The reason is that non-prescribed or illegal drugs and alcohol are used to "self medicate" ADHD. Ironically, taking ADHD medication may lower the risk for addiction to drugs and alcohol. This body of research merits review and is something to be considered in making a decision about whether or not to medicate.

We have also come to know that for Colin, medication appears to be the best. This may not be the case for all people with ADHD. The appropriateness of medication is something that a parent, and to the extent that they can participate in the discussion, a child, should discuss with a physician. Now that Colin is older and much more confident about advocating for himself, we have had discussions with him about taking ADHD medications. He has told us without hesitation that the medication works for him. He routinely takes a lower dose than his size and weight would suggest he needs, and he is still affected by sleep issues if he takes his pill too late in the day. However, repeated experience, not the least of which are those days when he forgets to take his pill, have indicated to all of us that he benefits from ADHD medication.

Going to advocacy boot camp
Fighting to keep a school open

Christmas was upon us. It was the first one since Charon had died. The consensus was that the year had been both horrific and wonderful.

We looked forward to the New Year feeling it would bring closure to both my sister's death and to the arduous journey we had been on to support Colin. We thought we could coast for a while and be challenged only by "normal" day to day family issues. We were so wrong!

We enjoyed a wonderful winter holiday concert watching Kyle take his place on the stage with his classmates. We loved Strathearn School and its mature community. For some time, we had tried to buy a home in the neighborhood. But houses in mature neighborhoods are hard to find and we decided to hold off until we could get the right house in the best condition we could afford. In the interim, we were still driving Kyle to school in a round trip that took about 40 minutes — something we needed to do twice a day.

Most schools send home a variety of notices. Transported in backpacks, they typically arrive dog eared and smeared with remnants of lunch, but rarely in their original pristine shape. They can be about anything from "hot dog or whacky hair day" to information about the next School Council Meeting. The most important notices arrive in envelopes.

That December, in with the morass of brightly colored notices about concerts and other holiday events, a letter was sent home from our School Board. I forget the exact wording, but the message was that the district was doing a review of the school's sustainability. The letter seemed so innocent. More concerned with the details about what our children would wear and how they would sing on stage at the holiday concert, most of us ignored the letter. What did sustainability mean anyway? What it meant was that the school was being considered for closure.

I was on the executive for the Parent Council for Kyle's school. The Council members touched base to see if the notice was important. We asked if there was cause for worry. We were told the notice was routine. In retrospect, the most serious mistake we made, and it was one of the few, was to ignore the importance of that initial letter. Another community with a school slated for possible closure rallied as soon as they saw the letter. By the time the motion to consider closure went to vote at a school board meeting, the community activism was sufficient to stave off a closure decision. We started too late, but we were mighty in what we did.

A fight to keep a school open has nothing directly to do with learning disabilities. But, it catapulted me into advocacy boot camp. It helped me develop skills and gain an understanding about education and its governance. These skills were completely transferable to the area of special needs advocacy.

The fight played out at public School Board meetings, in the media, and ultimately in our province's Court of Queen's Bench. Large parts of the process were ugly. Many reasons were cited to justify closing the schools. In our view, these justifications were spin doctoring. We felt that money was the primary reason behind the proposed school closures.

We had some appreciation for the pressures faced by our school district. The provincial government was unequivocal that there would be no capital funding for new school construction until a district's overall occupancy rate was above 80%. There were many new communities in the city that had no schools and the occupancy rate of schools in mature neighborhoods was low. To meet the 80% target, schools in mature districts needed to be closed; ironically, this occurred at the same time the city was launching initiatives to revitalize these communities.

It was like we were at war. Three of us were leaders in the fight. The president of our School Council, Deanna, could be characterized as the "mother bear" fighting to protect her children. The second member of our triad was Merilyn, a woman we lovingly called "Erin Brockovich." She was a tenacious researcher who was part legal fact finder and part master of detail. I was our policy person. Our skills were complementary.

The community was firmly behind us. Meetings took place in community halls, dining rooms, coffee shops and in the food court of the local mall. This happened in the days before social media. But we did make creative use of the parent council's portion of the school's website. We posted information to help people write letters to the School Trustees, along with correspondence any of us had received back from officials. The school board was initially oblivious to the innocuous link to the parent council's site from the school's website. When awareness dawned, we pointed out that the parent council website was resident on the web server which Paul and I owned. The district requested that we use a different visual theme to distinguish the parent site from the school site, a moot point, as that was already in place.

We decided there was value in joining forces with the other school councils to fight the closure process. I was the person delegated to contact people in the other three schools marked for closure to ascertain their willingness to work together. One school was resigned to closure, but parents from the other two schools were enthusiastic about forming an advocacy coalition. We became a team and the media was quick to pick up on the alliance.

We felt that the process used to consider school closures was fundamentally flawed. It pitted school against school, community against community, and was predicated upon a flawed consultation process. We were highly critical of the consultation process; we believed it to be structured to result in a predetermined outcome. But more importantly, we felt we were not being heard or respected. We also were suspicious that information we were receiving was being significantly filtered or was incomplete.

In order to gain more information, we initiated a request under the Freedom of Information and Protection of Privacy Act (FOIP). When we received information though the FOIP request, it was disconcerting to read documents where our motivation and character were called into question. We also saw how information we had requested had been "packaged."

Merilyn discovered that the School Board had failed to complete one of the steps in the school closure process outlined in the regulations. It was at this stage that the parents from the three schools decided to take the District to court for failing to follow the proper process. Four people stepped up to be plaintiffs; Deanna and Merilyn from Strathearn, and one from each of the other two schools.

At the same time, we tried to convince the elected Trustees that they should not close the schools. Our children made signs placed on lawns throughout the neighborhood and on major thoroughfares that said, "Save our School." We held rallies and protests — both around our school and outside the building housing the school board administration. We attended to details. Prior to the first protest, I phoned the Police Department to ask what we needed to do to make sure we complied with the law. The police officer I reached was amused by my inquiry, in fact he laughed out loud when I shared with him the purpose of my phone call. But, he did tell me how to make our assembly lawful. It was relatively simple and involved measures like staying on sidewalks, not stopping traffic, etc. We shared this information with our children. They were active participants; older children helped younger children. All were very careful about making sure our protest respected the law.

Throughout this entire fight, we sought to be examples to our children. Our focus was on process and policy. We felt elected Trustees should be accountable to the electorate. We were the electorate.

Shortly before our court date, I wrote a Letter to the Editor of our newspaper. It was published as the lead piece on the day our case was heard beneath a headline that read, "Court Case a Lesson in Civics." I wrote that the fight was not personal; it was based on principles. I wrote about how, in a democratic country, elected officials are accountable to the public and that we entrust them to make decisions. I said that as an electorate, we also have a responsibility to inform those who represent us about our views. In the instance we feel decisions by elected officials are the result of a flawed process, we have the right and responsibility to elevate that discussion to the Courts. I also noted that while elected officials deserve our respect and indeed admiration in running for office, they do not deserve our complacency. I said that these lessons were important ones for our children to learn, and it was for these reasons I was taking my son to court with me so that he could see this important aspect of democracy in action.

We won our court case. But, *we did not win the war.* And we basically knew we would not. The court case was held the day the School Board was to vote on the closure. For an hour, we naively thought our schools would remain open. However, the School Board immediately passed a motion to make an application to the government to extend the school year. This meant that they could continue to fight us through the summer.

Because of the potential for our plaintiffs to be exposed to financial penalties, the ongoing costs of the case, and the reality that inevitably the School Board would comply with the school closure regulations, we decided to drop the court case. The issue then immediately went to a vote by the School Board. They voted to close all of the schools slated for closure.

I was proud that we did not make the fight a personal one. I have strong negative feelings about the character of some people we encountered during our fight. But our public representations always remained on the process and its outcomes. We might say we felt that we were being bullied, but we did not call officials bullies. The distinction is subtle but important.

Perhaps the most important lesson I learned from our experience was that I could not expect other people, when presented with the same facts as me, to make decisions or draw conclusions in the same way that I might. This was a hard lesson. We expected that after we won our court case, the School Board would keep the schools open. We thought that they would capitulate rather than move the debate into the summer months. We were wrong.

When "fighting the system," as parents of children with exceptional learning needs frequently do, it is important, indeed vital, to consider an issue from the perspective of the people in the system. Their values and base of reference may be completely different. It is important to consider how officials may evaluate the facts.

Another lesson is that it is possible to fight "city hall." As a group of parent advocates, we made a difference. The next year, the School Board put a moratorium on closing schools and re-examined its closure process. The current process is not optimal, but it is light years better than it was when we battled to keep our school open. It too, has been shaped by parent communities who came after us and lobbied for change. They built on our work. Others will build on theirs. Though we lost our school, our actions resulted in change.

Our fight gave us all a crash course in media-relations. In the several months the closure battle raged, we made improvements in how we presented ourselves and our messages. Initially, we were somewhat unfocused and emotional. At the end, we took time in advance to decide upon key messages and how they might appear as sound bites. I also experienced my first media scrum! It is really hot when there are a number of TV cameras pointed at your face! And, yes, the camera does add ten pounds. But, as I learned to my horror as cameras caught me walking away from the Court House immediately following our win, they add 40 pounds when your jacket is open and the wind is blowing!

A shift in focus

The school closure fight was community activism on a scale I could not have previously imagined.

It was also situational. We did what we needed to do. None of us awoke one morning to say, "We are bored. Let's begin a fight with the School Board, involve other schools, and perhaps be part of a group to challenge them in Court!" The experience left an indelible mark upon me.

When Colin was four years old, in an off the cuff comment, a colleague said to me, "Now that you are a parent, I bet you appreciate your own so much more!" My response must have startled him. "I certainly do have a different view. Now that I am a parent, I cannot believe how they could treat my sisters and me the way they did."

Before Paul or I laid eyes on either Colin or Kyle, our fierce love for them drove us to be the best parents we could be. We are their caregivers, protectors, teachers, benefactors, cheerleaders, and more. Our mission is to support their growth to become adults who are happy, healthy, self-actualized people living life in an ethical manner to its fullest potential. I would step in front of a firing squad for my children. I know Paul would as well.

The experiences Paul and I had in our youth have influenced us in our role as parents. In many ways, my parents provided examples, for me, of what not to do. It made me resolute that I would be there for my children. I would be an active parent, supporting them and being there to help them live and grow and to celebrate this fact as a significant achievement. Our children are cause for celebration in our life. We are happy they were born.

As adults, I did not want them to say, "Mom and Dad ignored us." Or for Kyle to say, "Colin really needed help. I wonder where Mom and Dad were. It is a shame. There is so much that can be done to help people with learning disabili-ties." Or for Colin to say, "I was left on my own to cope with this disability. It was so much harder than it needed to be." When we made the decision to become parents, it was accom-panied by a commitment to be the best parents possible. Being an advocate for Colin and Kyle is something for which we are hardwired.

Parents worldwide advocate for their children. Yet there are degrees of advocacy. For parents of children with excep-tional needs, the role of advocate is extended — stretched to include addressing issues that result from exceptional needs. An analogy might be that of a long distance runner. Parents of children with exceptional needs are marathon runners; others are middle distance runners. Both require significant effort. But finishing off those last few miles of the marathon causes you to dip into reserves you may think you don't have. Somehow you finish the race.

Paul and I did not awake one morning to say, "We will have a child with learning disabilities. We will become his advocate." It was situational. We did it because we had a child with exceptional needs, and we were his parents. It was our job and his birthright for us to be his advocates.

Our journey of advocacy for Colin could have been made so much easier — if there was early identification of learning disabilities — if there was greater awareness about this lifelong disability — if support in schools was not based on a wait to fail mentality — if ...

Somehow, accidentally, I had been enrolled in a concentrated course in advocacy when I was involved in the school closure fight. I had become an accidental advocate. The awareness was growing in me that it was time to apply the skills I learned during the closure process to advocate not only for Colin, but for others like him. Others saw it too, and they told me.

I am not sure if the conversation was planned, but an exchange with Rob Cameron helped me decide what I needed to do next. Our discussion occurred on the front steps heading into Colin's school. The school is an old and gracious looking building. The steps complement wide double doors that lend the impression of entering a castle. It was a brilliant sunny fall day. We were speaking about our youngest son Kyle. His first school now closed, Kyle was in grade three at King Edward

Elementary across the street from Colin's school. Rob was the principal of both schools.

Rob was a bit cautious in how he introduced the topic. He said, "I would never wish for a parent to have a child with any disabilities. But you are the parent of a boy with learning disabilities. I have watched you, and anytime you speak, you always do so with consideration of the needs of all children. Maybe there is a greater reason for you to be where you are now. I would encourage you to think about a broader level of advocacy. You have the potential to help a large number of children. I think you could make a difference."

Gradually, somewhat tentatively, I began a new chapter in my life. Without abandoning the critical function of advocating for Colin, I began to shift my focus. I looked outward.

Going public

The universe wasted no time presenting me with an opportunity to adjust my focus to the larger picture. Within weeks of the stairway conversation with Rob, we learned our school district was initiating a program review on learning disabilities.

This meant they were going to assess the way in which the district educated students with learning disabilities and the manner in which those services were funded. I was a bit suspicious of the district's motives. The last district review in which I had been involved resulted in the closure of four schools. I was also not confident about the process that might be used to conduct the review, still reeling from the intense fight that had taken place, about process, with regards to school closure.

I was also naïve to a debate raging in the field of special education about the most appropriate venue in which to educate students with exceptional learning needs. This debate saw inclusionists square off against those who favored a more specialized approach for students with exceptional learning needs. Paul and I had been oblivious to this debate when we

elected to have Colin attend a specialized school. We based
our decision on what we thought was in his best interests
as a learner at that time. We had experienced an exceptional
inclusive environment for Colin in grade three. At the end
of that year, we all agreed he needed specialized support
to address his educational needs. The best place to get that
support, as far as we could determine, was AKE. But, this did
not mean we were against inclusive educational environments.

There was palpable concern expressed by many of the AKE
school community that the program review would surrender to
the political clout of the inclusionists and result in the closure
of the school. I was now the co-chair of the school's parent
council. With the backing of that group, I used my experience
writing to Trustees to communicate our concern about the
possible elimination of the special education program in
which Colin and other students were enrolled. The letter also
included reference to the total number of families who could
be potentially impacted by the elimination of the program
and the school — numbers that far exceeded those affected
by the acrimonious school closure fight the previous year.
We received written assurances from the board chair that
the district remained committed to its principle of choice.
We also received assurances that the program review would
not lead to the closure of AKE.

Our parent community, with me as part of that group,
became actively and intentionally involved in advocacy. We
created an advocacy policy, reviewed and adopted by the

parent council. We intentionally and methodically became involved in the program review.

District representatives were invited to provide information about the programming review to our parent community. We invited trustees and other community leaders to attend that session. On the appointed night, our school library was crowded with a collection of parents, professionals and elected officials. The session morphed into something none of us expected. After the district staff shared their information, the focus shifted to the parents. They spent two hours sharing their experiences and frustration about getting support for their children. They were impassioned and genuine. One trustee told me afterwards that it was among the most powerful events he had ever experienced in his role as an elected official.

We followed this up with a structured process to solicit input for the program review. On a Saturday, about one hundred people, comprised once again of parents, profes- sionals and politicians, met to discuss the issues impacting students with learning disabilities. We compiled the dialogue and submitted it to the district as input into the programming review. I wrote the report emerging from the workshop. Even though the report was intended to provide input into the district's review, it had a broader focus. It referenced the provincial Standards for Special Education, standards which the district was compelled to meet.

And so began the process for me of advocating at a more public level. These first few steps were initially tentative and somewhat symbolic. But they were important for a number of reasons. I began to self identify as an advocate for people with learning disabilities. But I also *publicly identified* myself in this role.

My initial public outing had actually happened a few months earlier during the closure process. With the exception of our family and some people close to us, very few people knew that Colin had been diagnosed with learning disabilities. It wasn't as if it was a big secret; we just chose not to shout it out to the world. We planned that in two years, Colin would be back at his old school and all would be fine. The school principal at Strathearn had told us about many students who had received support and had returned to become honors students. That was our hope for Colin.

It was not planned. I was addressing the School Trustees, in the Board Chambers, in front of television cameras and reporters, and with some level of frustration, openly challenged the district. I said, "You do many wonderful things as a district. My son has learning disabilities and is attending a district school and is being provided with exceptional support. Why can't this same standard be extended to planning around school closures?" I am certain that only Paul and I appreciated the significance of my comment. I had publicly disclosed that our son had learning disabilities and that we were the parents of a child with learning disabilities. The secret, so to speak, was out.

What I learned from the school closure process was that

in advocacy, it is unwise to be complacent. It is suicide to remain quiet. Quiet equates to acceptance. It is absolutely vital to have a voice, and to communicate clearly and with passion, in that voice.

It was time for Paul and me to join the chorus of other voices and to make it louder. It was time for us to emphatically state that people with learning disabilities are capable of learning and succeeding in life. People with learning disabilities deserve access to high quality education. They deserve to have a future, just like everyone else. But we could not join that chorus of voices and affect change for others and for our son if we viewed learning disabilities as the family's little dirty secret.

The melt down

*While we were fighting to keep Kyle's school open,
and I was taking those tentative steps in public advocacy
in the field of learning disabilities, life trucked along for
Colin. In comparison to when he was in grade one to three,
he seemed pretty happy!*

There were moments, of course. The life of every child comes
complete with crises and tragedies specific to their age. "He
isn't friends with me anymore!" "I didn't get invited to the party."
"I didn't get all my homework done!" "I forgot my lunch."
"I don't like those girls. All they ever do is talk about shopping
and clothes." Every parent hears these or similar comments.
The normalcy was a treat. We far preferred them to the previous statements Colin made before he started at the Academy
at King Edward: "Why can't I read?" "Why am I so stupid?"
"Why does it come so easily for other kids? It isn't fair!"
"I want to fly into the sun."

    For me, grades four, five and six for Colin seemed to pass by
in a blur. When we were fighting the school closure, Colin was
in grade four. The primary goals for that year were to improve

his ability to read and write and to enhance his organizational skills and strategies. These two goals remained dominant throughout grade five and six.

Colin's goals were itemized in a document called an Individualized Program Plan (IPP). In other countries or provinces, this plan may be called an Individual Education Plan or Program (IEP). We had input into the plan; we signed off on it once it was completed. Every year, we would revisit the document that would be revised based on progress Colin had made towards achievement of goals. Both Paul and I found the IPP a much more valuable tool than traditional progress reports. One important aspect of the IPP was that it also identified issues that could impact academic performance. For Colin, one factor cited was his anxiety.

As a pre-schooler, Colin was not anxious. In fact, even with speech and health issues, he was a happy, sunny and confident child. He was affectionate but not clingy. Quick to smile, he rarely got into trouble. His anxiety began to surface at about the same time he was being bullied and began to feel like a failure at school — at the beginning of grade one. It continued to ramp up as he felt more and more like a failure, specifically as he progressed through his early elementary grades. By the time he started at the Academy, his self-confidence was low and his anxiety levels were high.

Colin was and continues to be governed by a strong moral code. He does not like breaking rules. He wants to do his best. He wants to do the right thing. He judges himself far more harshly than anyone else might possibly judge him. When you are incredibly bright and sensitive, but impeded in your ability to do your job, i.e., school, because of misunderstood disabilities, yet you are insightful enough to know the extent of your failure, anxiety and lack of confidence can result.

Once Colin got to the Academy, his confidence grew. But, it was much more difficult to empty out the well of anxiety. Anxiety, bordering on panic, inevitably surfaced when Colin was called upon to write. While he loved reading, he struggled with writing. Extracting a two sentence written answer to a question was painful. His verbal recall was and remains excellent; however, he hated being put into a position to write anything. It was during a homework session involving writing that he had a meltdown.

I do not recall exactly what happened beforehand, but I remember with some clarity the actual meltdown. He yelled at me, which in itself was quite unusual.

"I have LD you know! It's hard!" And then he went on. "What is going to happen to me? I want to grow up, you know, and have a family. I will need to get a job if I am going to have a family. What can I do? I have LD. You keep telling me I am smart, but you are supposed to do that because you are my mother!"

I was faced with an upset son. The irony was that he had, with his outburst, uttered the exact fears I harbored at that moment. Would he be alright? Would he be able to thrive as an adult? Would he ever be able to be independent of Paul and me? What would happen to him in our information world if he could not write? Those questions caused both Paul and me, at different times, to lay awake at night lost in worry. I remember clearly, when he was in grade two, having a full scale panic attack in the middle of the night, drenched in sweat, worried about his future. It was like we could never die, because we would have to remain alive to watch out for our child. Those thoughts were not ones we shared with him.

Homework put aside, he settled down. I wrote a note in his agenda that he had tried hard, but had been unable to complete his work. But Colin's outburst did provide a hint about how we might support him. If he did not believe either Paul or me that he was smart and that he had potential, he might believe someone else, someone he respected. That person was Rob Cameron. I caught Rob on the steps of the school the next day. I told him what happened. I asked for his help. Rob said he would speak to Colin.

Neither Rob nor Colin ever shared with me everything that was said during their conversation. Rob did let me know he had shared a juice and a chat with Colin. But I was able to piece together snippets of the conversation.

Colin came home that day to say to me, "I think I want to be a teacher."

I replied, "That is really good, Colin. What made you think you might want to do that when you are older?"

"I met with Mr. Cameron today. We had a juice. He told me I could have his job," Colin noted. "We were talking about my future and stuff, and he said that I was very smart, and that I could do anything I wanted. He said that I could even have his job." Colin continued, "I like kids. I think I want to work with them, particularly kids like me who have disabilities."

Colin had always demonstrated an amazing ability to relate to younger children. Large and gentle, he seemed to attract little ones. When he was nine, he volunteered for several months as a worker at the YMCA drop in baby-sitting service. The job required that he get a police check. I remember with some amusement taking him to the main station with the completed police check form. We were directed to a counter, which he could barely see over. He gave the police officer his form, saying, "I need to have a police check so I can volunteer."

Colin's aspiration to work with children was something that made sense to me. Having a vision for the future was even more of a godsend. It meant our son was beginning to believe in himself. I was grateful to Rob beyond words because of the critical role he played in helping Colin to believe he had a future.

Stopping the hemorrhage

It seemed like a good idea at the time. But, when we look back, or more specifically, when I look back, I think to myself, "What was I thinking!" We were seeking solutions to the fact that Paul and I were hemorrhaging money.

I had been in a consulting role, successfully, since I left the hospital. I was also getting a bit lonely, and truth be known, a bit bored. I wanted a change — not a complete change, but certainly a bit of a difference.

The situation we faced with our consulting business was almost the result of a perfect storm. When Charon was dying, I was busy with a number of consulting assignments. There is a rule in consulting. You are always marketing or seeking new contracts. When you are working into the small hours of the morning, it is hard to think of the next assignment, but it is critical to do so. With the focus on Charon and Colin, I concentrated on family priorities. I did my work, but did not actively go after new contracts. I broke one of the cardinal rules of running your own business.

The other truism in consulting, at least in the public sector where my practice was concentrated, is that new projects do not begin six months before or after an election, though approved projects continue. In the year after Charon's death, we went to the polls in federal, provincial and municipal elections. People in the printing business made money, producing pamphlets and lawn signs. I was faced, for the first time ever in my consulting practice, with little business. And it was my own fault. I had violated rule number one and had been impacted by the consulting hiatus that resulted from three elections.

Paul and I decided it was time to change our focus. With his skills in computers and mine in data analysis, we elected to venture into a new market — online surveys. In a short period of time, we completed three major online surveys for clients. The work was very well received — in one instance it was lauded nationally. But, even here we experienced a wrinkle we had not foreseen. We had retained a consultant and paid him handsomely to do database work for us. When we proposed a strategy for profit sharing for future surveys, he advised us that he felt he owned the databases that we had paid him to create. We envisioned ourselves in court with him, a fight we could not entertain. We were spent, both emotionally and financially. We decided to pull the plug on the survey business.

We made the decision in late fall. At about the same time Rob spoke to Colin about his future, we were rethinking ours. We decided it was time to go back to salaried employment and planned to make the change after Christmas. Our holiday that year was quiet. The decision to move in a different direction brought with it some peace. Of the two of us, we figured I would be the best suited to return to a nine to five role.

I had thrived in the hospital environment. I had demonstrated I could work in large and highly political environments. Paul, on the other hand, had always felt like a round peg in a square hole in bureaucracies. Exceedingly smart, he had little patience for inefficiency.

The resumes were primed and sent off the first week of January. Events transpired at a speed that was surprising. With his computer skills, Paul sought work in the information technology field. Almost immediately, he was offered a position at the new Dell Call Centre that had opened up ten minutes from our home. It was shift work and the salary, given the position, was poor. It appeared to be drudgery in an environment that fuelled every Dilbert cartoon either of us had ever seen. Paul was inclined to accept the position. He thought it was important to support our family, to stem the hemorrhage of money. I was so happy when he agreed that the position was not the best fit for him. He advised the company that he wanted to delay the offer for a month. We figured that if nothing else surfaced, he might consider the job offer as a fallback. Coincidentally, the Call Centre would close 24 months later.

I applied on three jobs, two in health care and one as a research policy analyst role for the City, the latter being a position for which I was overqualified. I quickly secured interviews for the two health care opportunities. Now faced with options,

I made the wrong decision. One job had a slightly higher salary than the other and fewer staff to manage. I pursued that job opportunity. It seemed less complex, and I thought, naively, would enable me to spend more time with my family. It led to almost two years of hell that cost me dearly in many ways.

At the time I was in the midst of interviews, Paul applied with a high level of enthusiasm on a position at a college in Edmonton as an assistive technology specialist. When he had worked for the University, Paul had established an assistive technology laboratory. He also maintained close working relationships with the staff providing support services to students with disabilities. As a person with permanent after-effects from his spinal cord injury, a son with learning disabilities, learning disabilities and ADHD himself, he understood the human aspect of living with disabilities. He was quickly hired. It seemed like everything that happened in his life had been preparation for this type of work.

Paul started his new job one week after me. He spent that week teaching and then supervising our children on how to the use the public transit system. We were driving the boys back and forth from school. With our new employment situation, changes were needed. Getting Colin and Kyle to school was not an issue; Paul would drop them off on the way into work. He had negotiated with his employer for a start time that accommodated that reality of our life. But neither Paul nor I could pick the boys up at the end of the day. Colin, now in grade six and of a size to discourage anyone from trying to bully him, and Kyle, at the end of grade four but sophisticated beyond his years, were the first in their group to become bus savvy! Colin's teacher said that other kids in the grade six class were speaking about how they, too, would soon be learning how to take the bus. But in this social contest, Colin and Kyle were first off the mark!

My new job was with the Government of Alberta. I transitioned into a sea of office cubicles, even though I had a senior management position. My work station was very different from the private offices I had occupied during my salaried days at the hospital. Each little cubicle looked the same as all the others, with status dictated by proximity of the cubicle to the windows. I could not help but wonder how anyone with attentional issues, like Colin, could work effectively in such an environment.

I had amazing and dedicated staff. If there is anything I regret is that I no longer have frequent contact with many of these people. I took a position at the helm of a program that had been the focus of much derision by others. The program was criticized for not meeting its mandate or being service orientated. I launched into action, and almost immediately was reminded of the layers of branches and people that influence government operation.

I started the job in mid February. By March I was convinced I had made a big mistake. I tackled the job with my regular ferocity. We quickly made progress. While I encountered many kind, hardworking and very smart people, I also met some who were mean. They lied. They had gone to a school where they learned that in order to look good, it was imperative to make other people look bad. I felt like a fish out of water. But I was getting a paycheck. Between Paul and me, we were no longer hemorrhaging money.

On the radio!

A few weeks after I started my new job, there was a con-ference in Edmonton that focused on how inclusion was the best option for students with exceptional learning needs.

I was approached by the Edmonton Chapter of the Learning Disabilities Association of Alberta about whether Colin and I would consent to an on-air interview with CBC Radio. The debate was whether a student could be educated and thrive socially in a specialized education environment. The inclusion conference had precipitated the radio spot. I was now a Board member of the Learning Disabilities Association of Alberta (LDAA), having joined when Colin was in grade five. It was part of the commitment I had made to engaging in a more public advocacy role.

Colin was in the final months of grade six. The decision to do the interview was his. In discussing the pros and cons, we touched on how we, as parents, felt it was important to share our story with others. We also told him that while we believed he had valuable things to say, we would respect and support his decision if he did not want to do the interview. But Colin was enthusiastic about the opportunity. He had said on many occasions that he was happy to have received support at the Academy.

My next step was to seek approval from my employer. While I was not speaking about a government program, I would be in the public eye. I was very happy when they approved the interview, with the caveat that it not enter into areas pertaining to government programs and services. I was fine with those conditions.

Colin was amazing. He was eloquent. He used analogies to describe his struggle with learning disabilities. He shared insight beyond his years. He said that having a learning disability was like being up against a glass wall. You can look through and see what needs to be done, but the glass wall prevents you from doing what you need to do. It was not something he had ever shared with us. It was not rehearsed. I answered the reporter's questions from the perspective of a mother. Responding as a mother got me into a bit of trouble, sort of...

One of the most worrisome aspects of our journey of support for Colin was when he said, "I just want to fly into the son." Our sunny confident child was speaking about suicide at the age of eight. It was one of the defining moments of my life. When asked about what we thought about Colin's school, I said without hesitation that I believed it had saved his life. Almost immediately, I felt I had breached Colin's privacy. Most interviews take several minutes and a great deal of content is recorded. Only certain items are selected to be broadcast, and play time is measured in seconds. CBC played Colin's glass wall comments. They played the comments I made about the school saving Colin's life. I was upset with myself. I had not protected my son's privacy. I knew better.

The day after the interview, I was told by parents that they appreciated what I had said. One confessed to me, "We had a discussion about it at supper last night." By it, she meant suicide. She continued, "It was the first time we ever spoke about it. It opened up the discussion for us. Our son told us he had had similar thoughts. Thank you for having the courage to say what you did."

While I appreciated what this mother shared with me, I still felt guilty. I apologized to Colin about the breach of privacy. Yet again, he surprised me. "Mom," he said, "You never have to worry about what you say when you tell the truth."

A battered body

Summer that year was hot. Perhaps it affected the mood of the people around me. Three months into my new job, my boss exploded at me and did so publicly, outside my little cubicle by the window.

I actually forget the specific issue that prompted the tirade. But it was unjust and unwarranted. I was incensed because I had done nothing wrong. Yet, I was more disturbed at how my boss had elected to deliver the message of displeasure. I suspect my boss was angry because I had been nice to a person considered to be my boss's arch enemy. I was told by other staff that the blow-up was pretty commonplace and that I should just get used to it. One of my colleagues tried to give me much appreciated support after hearing about the cubicle-side explosion, telling me that she thought I was doing a good job.

I had been emotionally battered as a teen. I had absolutely no desire to be in an employment relationship characterized by emotional abuse. Paul was furious and wanted me to quit. To be told, "That person does that all the time. Just get used to it," was evidence that I was working in a pathological environment that tolerated insanity. I have been angry at staff in the past, but never would I yell at them, in private, or worse, admonish them in public. In the midst of discussing the behavior of my boss with officials in the organization, life once again "happened."

It was a Friday afternoon. I had been at a meeting a few short blocks away from my office. The plan was that I would go straight home from that meeting and enjoy a wonderful weekend away from my pathological work environment. Paul says that my work situation contributed to what happened. I am not sure that is true, but the event that followed provided me with an enforced period to think about my job and my life.

It was also one of those situations in which different worlds intersect. I was in the crosswalk advancing towards the parkade and my car when I saw my friend, Deanna, the person who had been our mother bear from the Strathearn School closure fight. Shortly after the schools closed, she had been diagnosed with breast cancer. I had seen her after she had been through a course of chemotherapy, just when her hair was growing back. As I crossed the street, her car pulled up to the crosswalk immediately beside me; she had a full head of hair! Thrilled to see her, I smiled and waved. In that instant of signaling my greeting, I did not, as I always did when crossing that particular stretch of street, look at my feet to navigate around the dips and potholes.

I suspect that I smacked down on the pavement in a manner that looked like I was a comedic actor in an Abbott and Costello show. My left foot caught the pothole, and twisted. I fell down face forward onto the hot asphalt. I have a memory of a person helping me up and then asking me if I was alright. I replied, "I am ok," and then immediately changed my mind and said, "No, I don't think I am. I need to sit down."

There is an entry to the underground portion of our city's light rail transit on the curb that had been my destination. I sat down on the low end of the concrete roof trying very hard not to pass-out. I was alone; the person who had helped me get up from the street was long gone. A homeless man came over to me. His warm and very much appreciated question, "You ok lady? Do you need help?" I was next door to the building that housed the Government's Department of Health and Wellness, at the end of a day on a Friday, and it was the homeless man on the street who tried to help me. I later thought that to be symbolic.

Deanna had witnessed the accident and somehow, in the midst of downtown rush hour traffic, had navigated her way to me. I did not know it was her at first, as she sat down beside me and also asked how I was doing. My arms and hands were stinging. I felt like I was going to vomit. Deanna asked me if I needed her to drive me home. I said, insisted in fact, that I would be fine. I did ask her if she could help me to my car and we piled into her vehicle, parked illegally, to drive the half block to the parkade.

Both Colin and Kyle were at a summer art camp. The plans were for me to pick them up, and then take our youngest to his friend's house for supper and a swim. My first hint that

I might not be fine was when I used my arms to adjust myself in the driver's seat to put on my seat belt. It is one of those unconscious movements we do all the time. I was struck with excruciating pain. My second hint was when I tried to sign out both Colin and Kyle from the camp and had trouble writing. I had been in contact with Paul, who sensibly wanted me to go to a hospital. I protested, saying it would be crowded on a Friday afternoon and I had no desire to spend several hours in the emergency unit to be told I was banged up. I knew I was banged up and thought the time would be better spent recuperating in the quiet of my own home.

Paul called our doctor. His office called me to tell me to get there immediately. I dropped both kids off at Kyle's friend's place and circled back downtown to my doctor's office. I love my doctor. I worked with him at the hospital, and in the family doctor lottery, we won the grand prize. I was adamant. I said to our doctor and to Paul, who met me at the office, "I just have soft tissue injuries. I will be ok. I have had broken bones before. I know how it feels." I refused to go get x-rays or do anything sensible.

Both men, I think, knew better than to fight me. My doctor sutured up my right knee that I had not realized had been split open until I got to his office. He examined my other battered body parts to say I had a sprained left ankle, no real worries, and likely a torn rotator cuff. Then there were my arms. My hands and wrists did not appear to be broken, but he mentioned that sometimes injuries have a way of "showing up" and that he wanted to see me on Monday. He gave me strict instructions to call him over the weekend if my condition changed for the worse.

I went to work on Monday. I will admit it was not the brightest move I have ever made. I was interviewing for an assistant on both Monday and Tuesday and did not want to postpone these very hard to set up appointments. I did not get to my doctor's office until Wednesday morning. By that time, it looked like I had taken part in a bad experiment with purple paint. I had extremely large bruises, looking like purple elbow pads on both arms. I had very artistic purple and blue bruises up the inside of both my arms starting in my palms that appeared as if they had been applied with a paint brush. I still could not push down using my arms.

"And what day is it?" my doctor asked when he saw me.

"Wednesday," I replied.

"And you were going to come back to see me, when?" he asked.

"Early in the week," I replied, adding, "And its only half way through the week."

"X-rays," he said, "Now. Wait for them and bring them back."

When I got back with the big brown envelope full of x-rays of various body parts, he slapped them up in sequence on the viewing screen.

"You made out like a bandit. You wrists aren't broken," he declared as he looked at the films of both hands.

"Hmmm, your right elbow is broken. You sheared off the radial head," he said as he flipped that picture up on the screen.

"What?" I eloquently replied.

"All be damned! You did the same to your left elbow, but it's worse than the right!" he commented.

What?" I stated again, like my voice was stuck on a bad section of an ancient record, skipping back and forth over the same words.

"I'm sending you to a surgeon," he said.

In a radical departure from my previous inspired responses, I asked, "When?"

"Now, if the one that I want you to see is in clinic. Otherwise as soon as I can get you in. Stay here while we make the arrangements."

This time, I did as I was told.

The surgery to pin my elbows back together occurred the next Monday, a week to the day after I was initially supposed to see my doctor. I planned to be back to work the week after. It was during that first week of post operative recovery that I thought I might need to take two weeks off work. When I saw my doctor to get a note for my employers, he looked at me as if I had suffered an injury of reason in addition to two broken arms.

"No," he said. "You will not go back in two weeks. Six would not be an unreasonable period away from work. You are staying home a minimum of three! I will compromise and write you a note for three weeks, but I will certainly not write one for two weeks."

It was like I needed some time for the adrenalin to dissipate from my system. The adrenalin was not caused from the accident, but the stress I was under at a job that was very unpleasant. I knew I needed to leave. But like when I was a teen, I wanted to make the move in the manner that would be the best for not only me this time, but for my entire family. I made that decision while sitting on the easy chair, my arms on two pillows, and a book on my lap, also propped up by a large pillow.

The kids across the street

The Academy at King Edward, the school Colin began attending in grade four, is an historic building. It was built in the early 1900's, and carries with it the splendor of the imperial looking buildings of that day.

The school would not look out of place if transported, intact, to a British town. It is a red brick structure, with turrets, high ceilings and expansive hallways. The inside steps are rounded and made of marble. There are rumors of a ghost living in the girls' washroom in the basement! It is impossible to traverse from the north to south end of the basement; the entire east-west core contains the fixtures and associated storage area for a long unused coal furnace! The main level of the school houses elementary aged students and the school library. The top floor is for students in junior high, those in grades seven to nine.

There were major changes afoot in the fall of the year Colin began grade seven. The district moved the principal, Rob Cameron, to another school. We found out about Rob's transfer the previous spring when Colin was still in grade six.

Rob called me early one morning, before I left for work, to give me the news. I was upset. First, and most importantly, I would miss him. I would miss his caring, his advice and the enjoyable hallway conversations. But, on a very selfish note, it was like our safety net was suddenly being eliminated. I exonerated Rob. Whatever the problem, I felt he could fix it. And Rob could not fix problems related to Colin's education if he was at another school.

It was also a year of transition for Colin. For two years, he had a wonderful teacher, a master at navigating the balance between tender and tough. Vicki, who taught Colin in grade five and six, had challenged him. But she was kind, and Colin continues to regard her as one of his "best ever" teachers! As a new grade seven student, he would be leaving her class and the main level of the school to go upstairs to Junior High! He would have a locker with a lock. He would be moving from one classroom to another. He would also be selecting options! It was going to be different.

I walked upstairs with him on his first day of grade seven. We checked out the names beside each door to figure out which class was his. The two of us carried large bags of supplies, many of which were designed to reinforce organizational and time management strategies. When we found Colin's home room, the two of us entered together to meet one of his new teachers.

Colin was apprehensive. When greeting his new teacher, he declared, "I'm a bit nervous. This is my first day of Junior High."

His teacher, not missing a beat, responded, "It's my first day

of junior high too!" Colin's body language signified a percep-
tual drop in his anxiety.

Those first few weeks of grade seven were notable for
being un-notable! Colin slipped into the junior high routine.
One of the most challenging aspects of this new environment
was keeping track of his personal belongings. In the elementary grades, each class came equipped with a cloak room for
coats and backpacks; students also got to store supplies in
their desks. Colin and his classmates would be moving around,
and their lockers became the central repository for everything.
In a school where a large proportion of students had ADHD,
the ability to keep track of books to pens to gym strips was
an uphill battle.

In late September, one of Colin's teachers caught me in the
hall. Circumstances that day had conspired to allow me to pick
him and his brother up from school.

"I wanted to speak to you about Colin," she began. "Do you
have a minute?"

We sat down on a bench that punctuated the large hallway.
She was concerned about Colin's self-confidence. She asked
if I had any ideas about strategies that could be used to bolster
his confidence. Anxiety, once again, was rearing up its head.

I told her about the meltdown Colin had experienced the
previous year, and what Rob had done to help.

"Colin told Rob that he wanted to be a teacher," I said,
"and he is particularly interested in working with young children
with special needs." I continued on, "He is actually really good

with the little ones. In fact, I think he relates better to them than he does to kids his own age."

With only the slightest of pauses, she inquired, "Do you think he might be interested in volunteering with the students in the Interactions Program?"

I replied without hesitation, "Absolutely!"

"Leave it with me," was the response.

The Academy at King Edward is part of a multi-campus. It is comprised of the specialized school for students with learning disabilities in grades 2 to 9. Part of the multi-campus also includes King Edward Elementary School located across the street from AKE. AKE also has a high school program co-located in a down town high school venue. The multi-campus falls under the administration of one principal. The Interactions Program, a specialized program for students with autism spectrum disorder, was sited at King Edward Elementary School. The teachers in the program were exceptional, and many of the students in the Interactions Program were integrated to varying levels in the regular classrooms.

A few days later, Colin came home to tell us that he was going to begin working with the Interactions students twice a week. Arrangements had been made for him to leave his classes on Tuesday and Thursday a bit early in order to go over and volunteer in the program.

Colin loved the opportunity. The days of the week were distinguished as "Interactions days" and other days. On those instances where he was unable, for some reason to go over on the appointed Tuesday or Thursday, he complained! He was able to learn more about autism spectrum disorder at a very practical level.

This became evident to me in the spring of his grade seven year. A man that I had met at my government job had a young son with autism. He was aware that Colin attended the Academy and thought I might know something about the Interactions Program at King Edward Elementary. I told him that I knew the teacher was excellent and that Colin was volunteering in the program. I said that I would ask Colin what he thought.

I posed the question to him that night. "Colin, my friend from work has a son that has autism spectrum disorder. He was wondering about whether the Interactions Program at King Edward would be a good choice for their son. He is ready to start grade one."

Colin, in very much a teenager kind of way, rolled his eyes. "Mom," he said, "kids with autism are not all the same!" He continued, "There are really three groups of students in the Interactions Program at King Edward."

I was curious as to what he would say next.

Colin went on, "There is a group of children who do not speak at all. It is a hard to communicate with these kids but they listen and they know what is going on. Sometimes they act out, and that is hard because it is not like they are being bad. It is just the way they are. The teachers are really good. They don't say, 'You are being bad.' Most of the time, the teachers try to get the kid's attention with something else so that they stop what they are doing. That is called redirection."

Colin continued. "There is another group of kids who speak but they have trouble with behavior that might not be appropriate. Some of the other kids at the school think that they are a bit weird, but they are actually fine. They sometimes blurt out stuff at inappropriate times. The teachers try to explain to them the best way to act. A lot of these kids also go into the regular classes at the school."

"And the third group of kids is somewhere in between the other two groups. They may not talk, but they act ok. Or they talk but act out a lot. What is your friend's son like?" Colin inquired.

I was somewhat dumbfounded at Colin's response. He had analyzed, from his 13 year old perspective, the characteristics of the students he was helping to support. He did it in with more insight than many adults I had encountered. Most notable for me was that he did not blame or assign shame to any of the students because they had autism. In a very adult manner, he accepted responsibility for selecting and then using strategies to interact with these children in a respectful manner. His actions and words were empathetic, underscoring that the students in the program had thoughts and feelings. While he may not have provided a comprehensive synopsis of autism spectrum disorder in that conversation with me, what he said for a 13 year old boy providing volunteer support two hours a week was quite sophisticated.

I shared with Colin that I could not answer his question about the way my friend's son acted. Colin then said, "The best thing for him to do is to come and see the program and then decide if it is the best for his son." Good advice, indeed.

With increasing curriculum demands, Colin's volunteer schedule dropped to one session per week in grade eight. His schedule did not permit him to volunteer at all in grade nine. But, the experience was one that he remembers fondly. It also was one that instilled in him some pride in being able to follow a passion, and work towards achievement of a goal, namely being a teacher.

Of World Summits and worry

*Colin was challenged by transition in grade seven. And,
I was challenged by the need for transition. When I fell
and broke my arms, I had an imposed time out.*

I returned to work after three weeks, working half days at the
insistence of my favorite family doctor. The three week hiatus
and the release of the final book in the Harry Potter series did
much to restore my mental equilibrium. It quickly evaporated
as I walked into my little cubicle to find all my plants dead.
The dead plants were somewhat symbolic to me, and absurdly,
quite upsetting. I rationalized it by saying that in my absence,
no one would have come by my cubicle to have noticed that
the plants needed water.

    I was also facing a conundrum. I was aware, as were the
people with whom I worked, that a new position would soon
be advertised for which I was ideally suited. I was being
solicited to put my hat into the race for that position. If I got
the job, it would mean that I would interface with the group
I now managed, but would lead a program at arm's length
from government. The field in which I worked was complex;

in a short period of time I had amassed considerable technical expertise. I was also seen as having the personality to make things happen. To me, it was the best of all worlds. I would have greater independence, be able to build upon my expertise, and continue working with many people I liked.

There was another complication that tested my resolve. In the fall, the Executive Director of the Learning Disabilities Association of Alberta, a man I admired, resigned. The LDAA, of which I was a board member, would be recruiting a new Executive Director. It was a part-time contract position. I thought seriously about competing on this opportunity, feeling it would enable me to marry my passions and skills. I was adamant about changes needed to better identify and support people with learning disabilities. A job as the Executive Director would enable me to really invest my efforts in advocating for necessary changes. Another positive — it would permit me to do a bit of consulting. On bad days at work, I had often joked and said, "Just make me the CEO of a non-profit!" That potential was in front of me to explore.

Paul and I discussed my job situation extensively. He was blunt about his feelings. "Get the hell out of where you are now. Don't wait for the other position." It was reminiscent of when I was encouraging him to leave the university.

I can be a stubborn person. I was also optimistic. "The new position will be different, Paul," I argued. "And the salary should be good." The sub-text, it will be the best for our family. I went after that position. I received the formal offer in late

December — six months after I had broken my arms on the pavement outside my office tower. I also agreed to sit on the search and selection committee for a new Executive Director for the LDAA.

The job was good at first. But, like the perfect storm that had influenced my consulting practice, it was beset by the same circumstances that had made my previous job miserable, complete with new and innovative sources of grief. I was still in physiotherapy to regain both strength and flexibility to my arms. The accident and surgery that followed seemed to sap me of energy. I was miserable, and worse, I felt powerless. It was like I was once again in my teens, but this time without resiliency. As I drove to work, I adopted the practice of playing inspirational uplifting songs, ones intended to motivate and inspire me to reframe my daily experiences. I can still recite the lyrics of Ordinary Miracle, a song sung by Sarah McLachlan. It was among my inventory of uplifting songs. I like Footloose as well, but rarely included it in my group of morning feel good songs as the beat just made me want to drive too fast!

I am conscious, in writing about my adventures in employ-ment, that I am bound by oaths of confidentiality. I cannot nor do I want to breach my ethical or legal obligations. But a flavor of the hellacious environment in which I worked might be gleaned from a criticism I received from a senior official, emailed to legions, which complained about my use of a different color font in one part of an email. I had used it to emphasize a change in location of a meeting.

I tried, or perhaps struggled during this time to keep up with my volunteer advocacy activities. In April, I attended the first ever World Summit on Learning Disabilities. Held in Lake Louise, Alberta, the event was chaired by Brenda Martin of the Foothills Academy in Calgary. The purpose of the Summit was to bring together world experts on learning disabilities. Representing diverse countries and cultures, consensus rapidly emerged at the Summit about the critical issues and actions necessary to maximize the human potential of people with learning disabilities. My role, as a volunteer, was to write a government white paper summarizing the consensus emerging from the Summit.

I love to write. It is a release. The process of writing also helps me clarify my ideas and analyze my world. I struggled to write the White Paper. It was more a reflection of my mood than my capabilities. I began to withdraw. I suspect that I may have been flirting with clinical depression. I was a person who had withstood a mountain of issues in my life. I was well regarded for having both talent and tenacity. All I wanted to do was shut out the entire world to the exclusion of just a few. In the meantime, I lathered about not having a draft of the World Summit report completed.

That summer, Paul and I decided to fly out with the boys to Kelowna to visit my family. Nancy and Sam lived just outside Kelowna, as did my father and the woman he had remarried. Dad and his wife had decided to move to Vancouver. Paul and I thought we could make the trip into a family vacation our sons would enjoy. Its timing was to coincide with a formal party my father and his wife were hosting to enable them to say good bye to everyone. We booked a vacation package deal, designed to give us time to play around water, sightsee and just hang out.

This expensive vacation now causes us some laughs though at the time it was not too funny. The van we rented moaned when it shifted gears and had a GPS stuck on Japanese audio playback. The water in the pool was milky; Kyle got a nasty skin rash from swimming that took forever to go away. The hotel room was so dirty that Colin suffered from asthma the whole time we were there. There were steps everywhere, making it a challenge for Paul to navigate around the grounds. And then, there was my father and his wife.

Even in my most depressed state, which was probably the condition I was in at the time, I am a pretty competent person. At the party, my father's wife asked me if I could hand out cards that would determine the order in which the different tables of people would go up to the buffet. I had previously experienced her mercurial nature, but was not quite prepared for what ensued. I did as I was told, or so I thought... how hard could it be to hand out cards?

Apparently, there is some complexity in handing out cards to ten tables of eight in a small hall. My erstwhile stepmother, in seeing me failing to meet her expectations, issued a correction, and of course, I modified my practice. But I was not fully in control. I was in a room full of adults, with a mean age of about 75, and some of them had their own ideas that were at odds with Dad's wife. Gasp, but some people went up to the buffet, out of order! They lined up a bit! Apparently, it was my fault.

Perhaps there was something in the Chinese calendar that said the years 2007 and 2008 were going to be periods of challenge and wackiness for me. I had been yelled at by testy bosses. I got dissed for using green font on an email. Now my father's wife was incensed because there was a lineup of three agile eighty year olds positioning themselves to get the best slices of turkey!

It had to happen. My father's wife then began to yell at me, in a booming voice that carried throughout the small hall, in front of 80 people, telling me I was doing it wrong and was ruining her party. It was like there was this contagious condition that rendered my parents, or those married to them, nuts.

In a strange way, she did me a favor. I think the absurdity of the situation snapped me out of the funk I was in. It gave me my fight back. I looked at her, gave her the remaining few cards, and then said, "Fine. Do it yourself." I also muttered something silently under my breath that would not have been appropriate for my sons to hear. I went outside the hall. Paul followed. His face was a bright shade of puce, his anger obvious.

"Let's go," he said. "Let's go back to the hotel, have a swim, get a drink, and get the hell away from here."

We stayed for the main course. The food looked good and we were hungry. But we left before dessert. As we were at the head table, our departure was evident. No attempts were made to apologize. It was as if nothing had happened.

Sometimes kids have the funniest way of achieving closure. In this case, Kyle was the one that made the million dollar comment.

"Why was Grandma so mean to you? Why didn't she let Grandpa speak?"

I said, "Actually, she is not your biological grandmother. My mother, your grandmother, died when Colin was just four weeks old. She is your grandfather's second wife."

"Well," Kyle sighed, "that explains a lot!"

I didn't have the heart to tell him that there might have been as much drama if his biological grandmother was alive.

Over the next six weeks, I got the White Paper completed. It went on to be tabled in the Alberta Legislature and the Canadian Senate. With Brenda Martin, Chair of the World Summit, I also presented it at the hearings for the National Strategy on Early Literacy. We also presented the White Paper at a number of conferences. I also promised Paul I would leave my job.

A TV role

It was fall. The LDAA was hosting a conference in Red Deer, a city located midway between Edmonton and Calgary.

The Red Deer Chapter of the LDAA had encountered some difficulties. The provincial association was organizing the one day conference to keep the Chapter alive and build awareness about learning disabilities in this central Alberta community. Logistics were being managed from Edmonton with the help of a conference planner. She was a dynamo at promotions, and had been able to secure a feature spot discussing learning disabilities on the local television station.

The hope was to video-interview a parent/child duo, the latter being affected by learning disabilities. I was asked if Colin and I would consider being the duo for the feature. Colin readily agreed. The piece was intended to serve two functions: to enhance awareness about learning disabilities and advertise the conference that would take place the following week.

The interview was conducted by Su-Ling Goh, a seasoned Global Television reporter and host of a recurring health segment. The focus was on the mental health implications of children struggling to succeed at school. Su-Ling and the videographer were highly adept at putting both of us at ease. Colin came across as a seasoned veteran. He answered Su-Ling's questions in a conversational, almost matter of fact manner. He spoke about how sad he had been when he was struggling to succeed at school. He spoke very positively about the move to the Academy and his improved reading ability. Colin discussed, with candor, how he had acted up from time to time when he was frustrated at school, drawing the link between behavior and emotion. I was so proud of him.

Before the interview, Colin and I spoke about off-limit topics. Colin indicated he had no problems with me saying anything. The point was to raise awareness about learning disabilities, and in this instance, its mental health implications. This time when I spoke about Colin's comments about wanting to fly into the sun, uttered when he was eight years old and frustrated with his ability to read and write, I did so with his blessing. I commented on the importance of addressing school issues and how it had a direct impact on mental health. The piece with Colin and me aired immediately after a segment on suicide. The impact of the two combined segments, and the message that failure to succeed at school might lead to suicidal thoughts was pronounced.

I saved the segment; it is embedded in a PowerPoint presentation I use when I speak to education students at university about approaching parents of children with exceptional needs. I reinforce the point that early intervention, attention to possible learning and health issues, could actually save the life of a child. The room tends to go quiet after I air the segment. I suspect that many education students have not considered their actions within this context. I suspect many teachers do not realize their potential life saving role.

I have now been interviewed a number of times, on both television and radio. When it is appropriate, Colin participates as well. It is interesting that at one point in our journey, I was reticent to share with others the fact that Colin is affected by learning disabilities. Colin is also very forthcoming about his learning challenges. Now I welcome the opportunity to speak on camera or radio as a chance to spread awareness.

When I think back to the difficult days when we were trying to discover what Colin needed to be a successful learner, I know both Paul and I would have appreciated hearing from other parents, like us, about the experiences they encountered. Speaking about learning disabilities is a vital factor in raising awareness about a condition which impacts, at minimum, one out of every ten people. We can all play a part in spreading the word.

A different role

I was adhering to the faint hope clause. I was hoping I might get a financial package.

The grant agreement to formalize the program I was entrusted to establish had not been executed some nine months after I started the new job. There was only a very faint hope it was going to be signed soon. But, package or not, I was leaving. I began to tell my friends and colleagues, "I am planning on leaving my job."

Their reactions were painfully consistent, responding with variations of, "It's about time!" or "Thank goodness!" or "Good for you!"

Their next question was inevitably, "What are you going to do?" My response was, "I am not sure, but likely return to consulting." The economy at that point was on overdrive, and the prospect of picking up contract work was excellent.

I told my colleague, Michele Pentyliuk, the President of the LDAA, that I would soon have more time and mental energy for volunteer work. I told her the reason why. Her eyebrows rose up a bit towards her white blonde hair.

"Really, that is very interesting," she mused. Michele's interest was a focused one. The contract of the Executive Director of the LDAA was ending; her thoughts were that I might be able to help out the association by transitioning into that role, even on a temporary basis.

I left the job from hell in mid November. I resigned my LDAA board position and entered into a contractual relationship with the association as its acting Executive Director. In March 2009, the position was made permanent. I now had the job I had been considering over a year earlier.

About a year before I left my job, I began exercising every morning in an effort to get fit and control my stress. I was not eating excessively or badly. But the weight was sticking to me like crazy glue. I was the fittest of fat people.

I continued to exercise every morning after I left "the job." I did not modify my eating particularly, except possibly to spend more time preparing food. Over eight months, the 40 pounds that gradually crept on when I started with the government, melted off my frame. I became a walking advertisement for how stress, and cortisol, can cause weight gain.

Colin and Kyle expressed their appreciation for the change in my life. They cut to the chase. "You are around more, Mom. You are happier." It was true.

I enjoyed my new role. It was a fit of passions and skills. Commitment to the mission of the organization made it far easier to work hard. I believed then, as I continue to believe now, that it is possible to make a difference, one person at a time. My touchstone and motivation — I did not want parents like Paul and me, with children like Colin, to go through what all of us had gone through. My position is not without challenges — all positions are, but on the whole, I think it is where I should be now.

The week after I left my job, the economy, which had been in overdrive, collapsed, effectively taking with it significant opportunities for contract work. But, I had one great and important contract. A poor economy was a bit of a speed bump, but not an insurmountable problem. I was regaining my resiliency.

Going social
LDExperience

In the fall after the school closure fight, I was invited to become an inaugural member of the Education Task Force of the advocacy group, Public Interest Alberta (PIA).

One of the online surveys that our company completed, before we pulled the plug on consulting, was for Public Interest Alberta. It was to assess the priorities and attitudes Albertans had about education. Over 4000 people responded to the survey, which, as might be expected with me as its author, contained a substantial segment on special education. It remains the largest ever survey on education conducted in our province.

The spring after I left "the job," I signed up to attend PIA's annual conference. Among the sessions I selected was one on social media. I knew it was emerging in importance and that it was critical I learn more. I was a social media novice. I was not on Facebook, could not figure out the appeal of Twitter, though I did conceptually understand blogs. I also intuitively appreciated the importance of social media for non-profit organizations. The speakers for the session were young, really young, but I was engaged and intrigued by what they had to say.

Of particular intrigue was the potential reach of social media. I had heard the term, "going viral," but had no real appreciation for what this meant. What it means is that each person, who sees something of interest, passes it along, electronically, to others, who then do the same thing. The growth curve or reach of going viral is exponential. Going viral might mean that a message can spread, in a matter of hours, to millions. I was also impressed that social media, on the whole, was relatively inexpensive. The major investment is time — the time it takes to participate. As a person now leading a non-profit, everything about social media was particularly appealing.

The week after the conference, I dipped my toe in the water and established a Facebook account. I was pretty stoked. Paul is our family's computer expert, which is both good and bad. Good in that I have access to an extensive array of IT devices and software, but bad in the sense that my own expertise is really limited to maximizing the use of software programs. Paul sets it up, and I use it!

I set up my Facebook account and got it going! I later learned he had an account that he had established just to check out the medium. He was not a Facebook user, per se, and was somewhat surprised when I announced to him, "I already have 24 friends...on Facebook I mean!" Of course, I also got books! I am perhaps part of the 0.5% of Facebook users who have ever looked at let alone read a book on Facebook.

I deliberately set out to use Facebook as an advocacy tool. In addition to my friends and acquaintances, I sought out decision makers and thought leaders, politicians, trustees, and others as my Facebook contacts. I also adopted a strategy whereby the majority of my Facebook entries were related to my role with the LDAA. I did however, on a periodic basis share stories and comments that could be considered personal. I found it to be valuable, yet another tool to get the message out.

I also started a blog. An Edmonton School Board trustee I admired wrote a blog about becoming and being a school trustee. The content was insightful, but her blog also had visual appeal. She had used a free blog service. I clicked on the links, and in five minutes, I had my own blog. In ten minutes I had a template and visual theme that looked good. Now all I needed to do was write something!

I thought it might be time to share our family's story — our journey of advocacy for Colin. So I just started writing. It was a cathartic experience. But it was also illuminating. I got surprised at where my fingers on the keyboard took me. There were times, in our advocacy journey, when I was angry. I actually don't like being an angry person. I don't like leaving anger to fester. It is destructive, at least for me.

In writing about our journey, I gained understanding. Importantly, I believe I gained insight into the limitations of the system and people with whom we had been in contact. I realized I was angry with many people — people who did

not have the skills that I thought they *should have* to do what
I thought they *should be able to do* for our son. Through writing,
I came to realize that these people, the focus of my anger, had
likely never had the exposure or training or support to do what
I thought they "should." Through the writing process, I forgave
many people, some of whom may not have realized I was angry
with them in the first place.

I started my blog in July. By August, I had completed 16
posts about our journey. I used Facebook to tell my friends and
acquaintances about new articles. They left comments and told
their friends. Pretty soon I started hearing, both on the blog
and off line from people who were regular readers of my posts.

William Radvanyi, a web developer and family friend
mentioned that the domains, LDExperience and LDJourney
were available. He knew how much I was writing, and suspected
I might want to capture my musings in a book. He suggested
I purchase the domains, and then post everything on a site
I owned rather than a service owned by someone else. Domains
are inexpensive, and I quickly snapped up LDExperience and
LDJourney. William offered to help me. I had some ideas on
how a website might be able to help people affected by learning
disabilities share their experiences. The vision of sharing stories
about learning disabilities became the central focus of the new
site, LDExperience.ca.

I was scheduled to be a speaker at the end of September
in Whitehorse in the Yukon at the national conference of the
Learning Disabilities Association of Canada. It gave us a target

date to complete the new site. I moved over the content I had posted on the first blog. I cajoled a few friends to write articles. LDExperience.ca was operational a few days before I left for Whitehorse, with its official launch date being October 1st.

William helped me by designing a bookmark to promote the site. It featured a picture of a wondering road, looping back and forth. I thought it to be symbolic of the journey of our family, and others, in living with and advocating for people with learning disabilities. We printed up a supply of the bookmarks, which I distributed at the conference and to my friends and colleagues. I was hopeful the site would be successful.

Technically, LDExperience is an "aggregate blog." Quite soon after it launched, the concept was proven. The site now attracts people from all over the world. Clearly, people appear to be interested in the personal and human side to living with learning disabilities.

I have also become far more adept at using social media to promote LDExperience. When a new article goes up on the site, I post a note about it on my Facebook page. I now tweet about it on Twitter!

Soon into my experiment with LDExperience, I started investigating Twitter. I initially thought, and pardon the pun, that Twitter was for the birds. But it has proven to be a remarkable vehicle for sharing information. I have now established Twitter relationships with people from all over the world who have an interest in learning disabilities and ADHD. We follow each other other's tweets, many of which include links to great online material. Twitter has proven to be an excellent way to spread the word about LDExperience and to let others know when there is a new addition to the site.

The mission of LDExperience has not changed since it was launched, though there have been some refinements. The site continues to profile stories about living with learning disabilities and ADHD, expert editorials, and an editorial column that I pen. It is, for me, a labor of love. Certainly, it was precipitated by love. I believe it has major potential for being part of the chorus of individuals attempting to spread the word about learning disabilities.

Good people and sleepless nights

This isn't about finding fault or assigning blame.
At the end of the day, if responsibility is to be assigned,
I will accept it to be mine. I became complacent.
Grade nine was a brutal year for Colin.

The difficulty began on summer vacation before the school
year even commenced. We wanted to get away. I wanted to
go somewhere close to water, where I could sit in the shade
and read. I wanted Colin and Kyle to be able to fish and snorkel
and generally kick back. I wanted Paul to have a place where
he could relax, enjoy the scenery and not be challenged by the
terrain. His balance is poor and uneven terrain is his nemesis.
I wanted the vacation we had not had the previous summer.
We also wanted it to be a low budget affair, which meant no
airlines and a destination within easy reach of our mini-van!
    I found what I thought was ideal. It was a small rental
cabin on the south shore of Pigeon Lake. Located an hour
south of Edmonton, we could bring food, Paul's canoe, and
just chill. The venue also met another of our goals. We wanted
to have easy access to a hospital in the event Colin's asthma

got out of hand — something that seemed to happen to him on holidays. The menu planned, the food packed, the books selected, we set out. The cabin was much more rustic than the pictures made it out to be. We settled in and began to try very hard to enjoy ourselves.

The first challenge was for Paul. There were several steps down to the lakefront. The nails on a number of the wooden slats on the stairs had lifted; the steps were treacherous for an able bodied person and extremely hard for a Paul with his mobility and balance issues. I worried for his safety. Exacerbating the problem was a loose hand railing. It would have easily collapsed had Paul needed to use it to prevent a fall. Every time Paul wanted to go to the lake, one of us walked ahead of him, his hand resting on our shoulder to help with balance and enable him to navigate the steps safely.

The lake had also suffered an intense out-break of algae which meant that the water was unappealing for swimming. But, in an optimistic frame of mind, we felt we were away from the hubbub and were intent on relaxing. We could work around the challenges.

Colin suffered. It was clear there was a mice infestation in the cabin; their characteristic stench permeated the place. Colin took meds to counteract the increasing tightness in his chest. A few days into the trip, we decided he should sleep in the cleaner sunroom attached to the cabin. But the combination of medications and weird shadows and noises in the sunroom kept him awake for the entire night. It completely destroyed his already tenuous sleep cycle.

We abandoned the rental cabin before our time was up. But that one night of insomnia wrecked havoc on Colin's sleep pattern for the balance of the summer. By the time he was ready to start school, he was having difficulty getting to sleep until about three in the morning. Then he worried about being able to go to sleep, and that, of course, kept him awake. He worried about school — the teachers had all stressed how important a year grade nine was and Colin obsessed on that remark, which I am certain was made in innocence. Because he was so tired, his resiliency was low and every little challenge became a major hurdle to overcome.

After school started, he began having panic attacks about the work. If the panic attacks became too bad, he would wake either Paul or me to seek reassurance. As September progressed, Kyle was the only one in our family who was sleeping undisturbed.

We connected Colin with a counselor in the hopes that might help. While the counseling sessions were not unsuccessful, they did not do much to erase his worries. The sleeplessness continued well into the fall term.

The teachers in his life were concentrating on getting all the grade nine students ready for high school. It was not as if they set out to increase Colin's stress levels, but the constant emphasis on how it was absolutely necessary to have this skill or that stressed Colin even more. Colin struggles in the area of organization and executive function, the very skills sets being emphasized as necessary to succeed at high school. What Colin heard was that if he did not gain mastery in this area, he would not be successful in high school. He extrapolated this to mean he would not be successful in life. His fatigue enhanced his worry. He worried more and that pushed back his sleep time even further.

We spoke to his teachers. They appreciated our feedback and did their best to frame their comments. It was clear Colin was extracting many statements out of context. But, it was up and down. He would frequently arrive home worried. During that school year, we had many conversations with his teachers about how he was coping.

In the midst of all of this, I was working with an expert panel of reading specialists. The LDAA was in the process of developing and piloting a screening tool, for use in kindergarten and grade one to identify children at risk for reading difficulties. A few members of that expert panel encouraged me to have Colin retested to assess where he was performing in comparison to his peers. It was not that I was resistant, but I was fairly confident that from a technical standpoint, Colin was getting all he needed at the school. There were very specific goals on his IPP relative to writing; consistently, he was demonstrating he was very proficient at reading comprehension.

Colin continued with counseling until mid winter. He was quite honest with me about the experience. "Mom, the counselor is really nice and it is good to speak with him but I don't really think it is doing me much good. I am not sleeping any better, really." We decided to take a break from the counseling. We were also, like many other services, paying for it out of pocket. It was not an insured service.

Then there was school work. Colin continued to experience his regular panic about writing. Paul had solutions. As a person immersed in the field of assistive technology, he had many technical solutions that would help Colin write; we had access to a full range of assistive technology. Paul was very knowledgeable and routinely conducted assistive technology assessments for students at the college where he worked. But Colin's attitude made it difficult for Paul to help his own son. Colin was resistive.

"Those are *your* solutions, Dad. They are not *my* solutions. I have different needs!" Paul and I could not help but think, "Why, oh, why is he being a resistant teenager on this particular matter?" Much to our frustration and that of his teachers, he was very resistant of any assistive technology solutions.

Paul had another practical idea. He thought it might be a good idea to bring in a learning strategist, someone who was neither his teacher nor his parent to work with him to assess his needs and identify strategies to tackle the work causing him so much stress. We discussed this possibility with Colin, and he was enthusiastic. When I had organized the sessions on the learning disabilities program review, I met a learning strategist who worked primarily with students with learning disabilities. I punched out a quick email to her to inquire if she might be interested in meeting with us.

Two weeks later Joan met with Colin. Joan is a practical and insightful woman. But more importantly, she clicked with Colin. It was the latter part of grade nine and Colin and his classmates were in the process of preparing for their Provincial Achievement Tests (PATs), something that had put him into a state of panic. The PATs carry with them all the negative consequences of high stakes testing. Schools are all too frequently evaluated on how well students perform on the PATs.

Colin came home saying it was critical for him to do well on the PATs. My reply both surprised and frustrated him. "It is important for you to *try* to do your best on any test. The PATs are no more important than any other test you have in the school year. Do your best certainly, but don't worry about them more than any other test."

"Mom, you don't understand. These are the most important tests! I have to do well!" cried Colin.

Unfortunately, I understood only too well. "Colin, the reason all the schools get worried about the PATs is that it is the test the government uses to try to figure out how well the schools are doing. You should always try your best, but please don't let the pressure get to you." Colin knew that I was quite familiar with the politics of education in our province, and wanted, I think, to believe me. But, like many other students writing high stakes tests throughout the continent, he felt the pressure.

Joan set out to help Colin prepare for the PATs. She used it as an opportunity to identify and implement strategies *that worked for Colin.* As Colin worked with Joan, strangely, the time when he nodded off to sleep got earlier and earlier. It was also an exercise of empowerment. Colin would schedule appointments with Joan based on his school agenda. "She knows how I think, Mom," he said. We had hit a home run.

In the midst of this, my friend once again brought up the value of testing Colin. We deferred to her wisdom. We arranged for Colin to have a test that would gauge his performance in a number of academic areas. The results helped to explain why he was having such a difficult time with grade nine.

His ability to decode was just slightly above the 20th percentile, at approximately a grade four level. His reading comprehension was roughly equivalent to a university under-graduate student. The tester indicated Colin was having difficulty decoding multi-syllabic words. She advised us his reading comprehension would have been at a higher level except for this particular difficulty.

The conclusion was he had been muscling through the syllabus on the power of his excellent verbal recall, something that was becoming more difficult to do as the course material became more demanding. His reading ability and comprehension for the words he knew were exceptional, but he was experiencing considerable difficulty in decoding, i.e., reading, the complex terms peppered throughout the grade nine text-books. This problem had likely been building for a while as he progressed to more complicated and involved curriculum, contributing to his stress. With the increasing complexity and volume of words that he needed to read, the weakness in decoding negatively impacted his mastery of the text. While his verbal recall was still excellent, it wasn't enough.

I shared the test results with the school administration. Colin had over a 60 percentile point difference in his reading comprehension and his ability to decode. It would have been easy to have assigned blame to the school and its teachers. In truthfulness, there was a period during which I felt duped and angry. I was distraught over the implications of the testing.

Once again, clarity came to me through the writing process. I realize that it was a situation in which we all learned a lesson. Colin is extremely bright, as are many people with learning disabilities. It is easy to be lulled into a false sense of security when dealing with people who are highly intelligent. The compensatory strategies bright people use may mask other underlying difficulties. With such obviously high reading comprehension, it was not intuitively obvious Colin was failing to decode multi-syllabic words. It was a similar situation to those times I took Colin to the hospital with bi-lateral pneumonia. He looked healthy. The doctors, gazing at a seemingly robust boy, thought he was healthy. It was only upon very specific investigation that they realized he was ill with a serious lung condition.

The other lesson was mine. I like the people at Colin's school. They are good individuals who try their best. I had complete and unfailing belief in their collective abilities. I assumed they would be fully aware of *all* of Colin's educational needs. I assumed all those educational needs would be met.

I am certain the teachers believed they were doing everything they should for Colin. But, in the same way that doctors had been duped by Colin, believing him to be well when he wasn't, his teachers missed the issues around decoding. Both Paul and I made assumptions his needs were being fully met. We had let down our guard.

In some respects, it is easier to advocate for a child if it is obvious their needs are not being addressed. Ironically, it may be easier if you do not like the people who are the focus of your advocacy. When you both like and trust the people who are supporting your child, advocacy becomes more complex and layered. It is easy to put on blinkers. When things do not go according to plan, it can feel like you have been betrayed and hurt. Rarely are things black and white. Even people who do good work miss important details. We discovered this when Colin was in grade nine.

Colin is now getting the support he needs to improve his decoding skills. We are paying for that support privately, adding to the already considerable amount of money we have invested to supplement his education in a public system. Lesson learned, we think we are back on track.

What is going to happen to them?

Colin did very well on his PATs and was proud of his accomplishment. Kyle ended up the school year on the honor role and very excited about an award in art! We were proud of both our sons!

We played it safe and took a cue from the two previous summers and made no elaborate vacation plans. Paul took a few weeks off and we did things as a family in our own community. Paul's sister flew in from Ontario and we had some fun showing her the sites around our city.

My sister Nancy and her husband Sam decided to fly both boys out to Kelowna, separately, for a visit to see them. Kyle was first up. While we had flown together as a family, neither Kyle nor Colin had ever flown on their own. Kyle was a bit nervous, but handled the airplane trip and time away from home like a seasoned traveler. The scheduling of Colin's trip to visit Nancy and Sam was made a bit complicated because Colin had a volunteer job that summer!

Colin remained true to what he had said to Rob Cameron in late grade six. He wanted to be a teacher, preferably to little ones with special needs. His summer volunteer job was very much focused on his longer-term goal of being a teacher. But, it also served another valuable function. When you are in the stage between being too young to have a part time job but too old to attend summer camps, it is easy to have a long and boring summer. Colin's volunteer job provided needed structure and focus for the summer months.

When Colin was still in grade four at the Academy, our parent council received a flyer from an organization that provided summer camps to children with a variety of exceptional needs. As parents, we all agreed it was difficult to find options for quality recreation for our children. We all had experiences where summer camp leaders had failed to understand and be sensitive to the needs of young people with learning disabilities and ADHD. Paul and I decided to try out this new camp, and enrolled Colin. It was run by an organization called AdaptAbilities.

Colin loved the camp. He appreciated its diversity and age range. Many of the campers were like him, while others had more severe physical, cognitive and emotional needs. Now Colin was set to go back to the camp as a volunteer leader.

In order to get the volunteer position, Colin had to complete an application form and provide references. His principal and the teacher-supervisor from the Interactions Program served as his referees. It was decided the best placement for him would be with the younger children, those who were six to nine years of age. Colin attended an orientation session with the salaried camp leaders the Saturday before the camps began. He was quieter than normal; his intensity was obvious.

The AdaptAbilities summer camps are located at two venues. The majority of the camps are situated in a large combined elementary-junior high school. AdaptAbilities also has an office and respite centre, located in a converted home a block south of the school. The plan was for Colin to work out of the office-respite centre site.

I drove Colin that first day. But we had planned it so that Paul would drop him off in the morning on the way into work and Colin would then take public transit back home at the end of his shift. He was nervously quiet. I walked in with him. We were both warmly greeted by a camp leader. Colin was made to feel very welcome and wasted no time interacting with the children who were arriving for the camp. I wished him good luck and was on my way.

Just a few minutes before noon, he called me.

"Mom, this is really hard," he said. "It is a lot harder than I thought it would be."

"Colin," I replied, "the first day is always the hardest. It will get better, I'm sure. Just hold in there. Are you having a lunch break?"

"Yes," he replied. "I am in the staff room. Mom, could you come pick me up today? I know I am supposed to be taking the LRT, but could you pick me up?"

I heard in that request, not a 15 year old, but a somewhat overwhelmed young kid. "I would be happy to pick you up Colin."

"Thanks Mom. That's great. Love you."

I was left, after the conversation, wondering if he was too young to do work of this nature.

Two hours later, the phone rang again. "Mom, it's me. I think this is beyond me. I don't think I can do this." The disappointment in his voice was obvious. "Can you come and get me? I'm at the school."

As I drove the short trip to the school, I was filled with angst. I did not want this to be a failure for Colin. This carefully selected volunteer opportunity was intended to be a win for Colin. He was to work in an area where he was known to have exceptional skills and one that he thoroughly enjoyed. After the difficulties he experienced in grade nine, I was afraid another failure might shatter his already fragile self-confidence. I was hoping there was a way to make it work. I walked into the school and quickly found one of the camp leaders.

"I'm here to pick up Colin," I said.

"He is in the gym with a group of kids right now," was the reply. I had half expected a response like, "Great, he is waiting for you ... he is anxious to see you." I certainly did not expect to hear he was still working.

The camp coordinator then said, "Colin is amazing." I had a surprised look on my face. I told her that I had received two somewhat panicked calls from him where he questioned if he could do the work.

I asked if she would be willing to speak to him with me. She collected another camp leader who had worked with Colin that day and we walked over to the gym to meet him. Colin saw me and motioned that he would be with us in a moment. He was sitting on the ground with a group of kids, smiling at them, engaged in conversation and games. He finished up and came over.

"You ok, sweetie?" I asked.

"Oh, mom! This is so hard!"

"Let's talk," was my reply.

The four of us walked over to an open area across from the gym that had a number of benches. The camp leaders demonstrated as much concern and empathy for Colin as they would for any of the campers. I was impressed and touched.

Colin repeated how hard it was.

One of the camp leaders said, "Colin, you have a gift. It is like you have this calling. You are absolutely amazing with children. I cannot believe that you are only 15. There are many adults who have worked with us who are not as good as you are with children. This is only your first day."

Colin looked at her, somewhat disbelieving.

"Colin," I said, "There is nothing wrong with saying you are overwhelmed and need help. That is actually a sign of maturity," I added.

One of the camp leaders added. "It normally takes older volunteers until the third day before they will say they are overwhelmed. You are asking for help sooner. That is a good thing."

The four of us continued to have an intense dialogue. I looked at him and said, "Being a volunteer is meant to be win-win. The organization benefits from the services you provide. You benefit from being able to learn and do something you like. Maybe what we need to do is figure out some different arrangement that would work for you and for AdaptAbilities. That way you could still continue to volunteer." Colin looked at me with intensity. I said, "Do you think it might be better if you only worked half days?"

Colin's response was immediate. "Yes. I think working a full day is a bit too hard right now. Half days would be better." And then he started to advocate for himself.

"I think it would also be better," he said looking at the camp leaders, "if I worked with kids who don't have really serious behavior issues."

Colin clarified that he found it difficult to know how to respond to the children who really acted out. It was not about the children, but his ability to deal with these children.

I learned a bit more about his day and the reason why it had been difficult. A child, affected by Obsessive Compulsive Disorder (OCD) had become obsessed with Colin. Colin is big and gentle and many young children seem to feel secure and protected around him. He tends to fit the stereo-type of a gentle giant. The child screamed continuously and could not bear to have Colin out of his line of sight. Colin is bothered by loud and continuous noises. He also felt that he was doing a poor job interacting with this young camper and meeting his needs. The camp leaders had thought he was displaying amazing skills. It was easy to understand why Colin was both stressed and felt out of his depth.

"Would it be possible for me to work with just one or two kids each day rather than a larger group?" he inquired.

"Absolutely!" The response was immediate and positive.

"Could we look at the list and figure out which kids I could work with?" Colin asked.

The association had assembled a document for the camp leaders that provided a brief synopsis of each camper, including their age, goals for the camp and a bit of information about any disabilities or medical conditions. It was like a mini-individualized program plan. Colin reviewed the list with the camp leaders, beginning a process of rapid fire questions.

"What is OCD?" he asked. We explained what OCD was, and how it had been reflected in the behavior of the camper he had worked with that morning.

"It says this kid has Tourettes. What is that?"

I responded by reminding him of a boy he had met who had Tourettes. We described how people with Tourettes might have physical ticks and jerky movements. We also mentioned how some people with Tourettes may blurt out profanities or negative statements, something over which they had little control. Reminded of the boy he had met with Tourettes, Colin nodded in understanding.

"What is SPD?" he asked quickly, moving down the page of the list of campers.

"That stands for Sensory Processing Disorder," I said. "People with SPD tend to get overwhelmed by sensory stimuli going on around them. I suspect that you might have a bit of SPD going on with you."

The questioning continued, like we were involved in a university seminar on exceptional needs. He skipped over a reference to autism. He was familiar with that condition.

"What does FASD stand for?" he demanded.

I answered. "It stands for Fetal Alcohol Spectrum Disorder. It is a very sad thing. It is a permanent brain injury that occurs when a mother drinks alcohol when she is pregnant."

"Why would anyone want to drink when they are pregnant?" he demanded.

"That is a good question, Colin. I just don't know, but it happens."

"It says this child has speech and language delays. What does that mean?"

"Speech and language delays are often early signs of learning disabilities, Colin. You had speech language delays when you were very young."

The camp leaders and Colin settled on some children with whom he could be partnered for the remainder of the camp. The leaders took the time to share a bit about each of these children, emphasizing in each case how wonderful each camper was.

He looked at the camp leaders, leaning forward towards them from his position on the bench.

"Can you introduce them to me now? Can I please have a bit of a tour of the areas in which I will be working?"

"Absolutely, Colin!" replied the camp coordinator.

Then he quickly turned to me. "Mom, I know I asked you to come pick me up to drive me home. But, I think I should really get comfortable taking the LRT. Could you walk over there with me and make sure I get on it ok?"

I was starting to feel that the day, which for a time seemed like it might be a disaster for Colin, was morphing into a major success.

We took the tour and Colin was introduced to the campers with whom he would be paired the next day. One little girl with severe physical disabilities lifted her hand when she was introduced to Colin. He gently gave her a "high five."

Colin's backpack was still over at the AdaptAbilities office a block away. We set out into the bright summer sunshine for the quick walk to the house.

Colin was quiet for a minute. Then he looked at me.

"Mom, some of these kids are really disabled. What is going to happen to them when they are adults?"

I paused for a minute before I answered. It was so critical for my response to be perfect.

"Colin, a good teacher often makes the difference between some of these kids being dependent or independent when they are adults. It is all about working with children who may have disabilities to support them to be as independent and self sufficient as possible. That is why teachers are so important. Your goal of being a teacher is important." I added. "Being a volunteer, what you are doing now is important. So is a smile and being kind and positive."

He continued to be quiet as we navigated the path from the school to the cross-walk. It was obvious he was thinking.

He looked at me and said, "How have you coped with me?"

I struggled to compose myself as I felt the tears beginning to well in my eyes. I did not want him to see me crying. I thought it might lend the wrong impression. I carefully chose my words, wanting them to say exactly what was in my heart.

"You were always a joy, Colin. You are a joy."

Loose threads

Before and while writing this book, I spoke to Colin and Kyle about whether they were comfortable with me sharing details about them and our family.

Colin was very supportive. The one worry he expressed, "I am the centre of attention. I don't want Kyle to be left out." I spoke with Kyle as well, explaining the purpose of the book. I said he was mentioned but the major focus was on how we had advocated for Colin. His response to me, "I'm fine with that Mom."

Colin continued to volunteer at AdaptAbilities the summer after grade nine. He worked half days, every second week. As the camps and his volunteer job ended that summer, the Executive Director of AdaptAbilities called me to tell me how successful she believed Colin's volunteer experience had been, and how kind and caring a young man he was.

In addition to his summer volunteer job at AdaptAbilities, in the summer before grade ten, Colin worked extensively with Joan to do some advance work to prepare for high school.

At the end of the summer, Colin flew out to Kelowna to visit Nancy and Sam.

Colin left the specialized educational venue of the Academy at King Edward at the end of grade nine. He entered grade ten at a high school relatively close to our home. Accommodations and supports were organized to maximize his potential for success. He is taking classes in a fully integrated environment with other high school students and is enthusiastic about the school and the supports he is receiving.

Paul continues to work in assistive technology and remains a strong advocate for people with disabilities. His mission is to provide students with appropriate technical supports that reduce barriers to education.

Kyle was identified as being gifted. He received accommodations for this exceptional educational need in an inclusive setting in grade four through six. He elected to enter a challenge (honors) program in junior high. He has a healthy and balanced outlook towards school. He is an avid artist and has begun writing in the science fiction genre.

My father, when we were young, used to joke about leaving home without a forwarding address. He and his wife are estranged from our family. In his periods of lucidity from his dementia, he had chosen to shut himself off from us and his only grandchildren. He and his wife moved without providing my sister or me with a forwarding address.

LDExperience is well established with the average number of visitors and page hits growing daily. It continues to be a large focus in my life.

I remain committed to working towards enhancing the

awareness of people with learning disabilities through my roles with the Learning Disabilities Association and other organizations.

I love writing. I plan to continue to express my creativity through the written word.

Acknowledgements

Writing a book may be a solitary activity, but creating a book involves a team. I have been supported by some amazing people during the period of conceiving, writing and finalizing *An Accidental Advocate*.

My family, particularly my husband, Paul Reid, my sister Nancy Popovich and her husband Sam, have been stalwart supporters. They have been there for me as I experienced the emotional highs and lows of writing my first book.

I am blessed with a number of dynamic, compassionate and intelligent women in my life. They were an integral part of *An Accidental Advocate*. The help and friendship provided by Kieran Leblanc has been pivotal. Thank you seems insufficient to convey my appreciation. Lori Fankhanel, in both her role as reviewer and cheerleader, was unfailing in her support. I hope I can do the same for her when she writes her book. Judy Craig has been a wise and unfailing support to me. I value her counsel. Michele Pentyliuk has been a stalwart supporter, and an individual whose advice I value highly. I am so grateful for the support from Jodine Chase, Lorrie Goegan, Linda Siegel and Diane McLaren. Thank you for taking the time from your busy lives to read the manuscript and provide me with your insight.

Thanks to Stephen Murgatroyd for your advice and support at critical times, and for reading and commenting on the manuscript. To Fil Fraser, it was wonderful to meet you through the book. Thank you for your contributions. To William Radvanyi, thank you for having the insight, a few years ago, to suggest the creation of LDExperience, just in case "you want to write a book!"

Natalie Olsen is a book designer extraordinaire. Thank you for your major contribution. To Xanthe Couture at Sextant / Cambridge Strategies, thanks for your feedback on the book, editing and support.

And finally, my sincere gratitude to Ken Chapman for his support, confidence in me to write a book and embark on this journey, and decision to publish *An Accidental Advocate*.

About the author

Kathryn Burke was born in Montreal, Quebec. She earned an honours undergraduate and graduate degree in Sociology from the University of Calgary. She has held senior management roles in hospital administration and health policy, and has undertaken numerous consulting projects in the fields of health and human services.

Kathryn has been active as a volunteer throughout her entire adult life. She joined the volunteer community dedicated to raising awareness and providing support to people with learning disabilities shortly after her son was diagnosed. She has served as a Director and Vice President of the Learning Disabilities

Association of Alberta. In late 2008, she transitioned into the role of the Association's part-time Executive Director, a position she continues to hold. In October 2009, Kathryn launched LDExperience.ca, a website created to help people affected by learning disabilities share their experiences.

Kathryn Burke lives in Edmonton, Alberta, Canada with her husband Paul and her two sons, Colin and Kyle. *An Accidental Advocate* is her first book.

Kathryn may be contacted at kathryn@LDExperience.ca.

About LDExperience.ca

LDExperience is a website established to support people affected by learning disabilities to share their experiences. The site
is accessible at either LDExperience.ca or LDExperience.com.
Launched on October 1, 2009, the site has attracted visitors
from all over the world. Kathryn Burke is the site's founder and
editor.

LDExperience features a column by Kathryn Burke on issues
associated with learning disabilities and special education. A
section of the site contains editorials penned by experts and
thought leaders in the fields of learning disabilities, Attention
Deficit Hyperactivity Disorder, Sensory Processing Disorder and
other exceptional needs. A popular segment of the site contains
stories written by people living with learning disabilities or
supporting those who do.

Kathryn Burke established LDExperience in the hope that
visitors, whatever their role, would gain personal insight about
their unique journeys. She welcomes articles from individuals
who wish to share their unique experiences.